Dag Hammarskjöld

left behind the manuscript of this book to be published after his death. It is a remarkable record of the spiritual struggle of a very private man who spent many years in the public eye, most notably as Secretary-General of the United Nations.

Markings

was first published in 1964, four years after Hammarskjöld's death. Almost thirty years later, it has sold over a half-million copies in hardcover and endures as a spiritual classic, read and reread by many who find insight, comfort, and inspiration from Hammarskjöld's poems, notes, and observations.

This fascinating self-portrait of a renowned peacemaker conveys the severity with which Hammarskjöld marked his own spiritual conduct and measured the integrity of his soul.

Other BALLANTINE/EPIPHANY

Markings

Dag Hammarskjöld

TRANSLATED FROM THE SWEDISH BY
LEIF SJÖBERG & W. H. AUDEN

WITH A FOREWORD BY
W. H. AUDEN

BALLANTINE BOOKS • NEW YORK

Translation copyright © 1964 by Alfred A. Knopf, Inc., and
Faber and Faber, Ltd. Foreward copyright © 1964 by W. H.
Auden.

All rights reserved under International and Pan-American
Copyright Conventions. Published in the United States by
Ballantine Books, a division of Random House, Inc., New
York, and simultaneously in Canada by Random House of
Canada Limited, Toronto.

Library of Congress Catalog Card Number: 64-19087

ISBN 0-345-32741-1

This edition published by arrangement with
Alfred A. Knopf, Inc.

Printed in Canada

First Ballantine Books/Epiphany Edition: January 1983
Sixteenth Printing: December 1993

Originally published in Swedish as *Vägmärken*. © Albert
Bonniers Fölag AB 1963.

Excerpts from this book appeared in *The New York Times
Magazine*.

After Dag Hammarskjöld's death, the manuscript of *Vägmärken* was found in his house in New York together with the following undated letter, addressed to the Swedish Permanent Under-Secretary for Foreign Affairs, Leif Belfrage.

✳

Dear Leif:

Perhaps you may remember I once told you that, in spite of everything, I kept a diary which I wanted you to take charge of someday.

Here it is.

It was begun without a thought of anybody else reading it. But, what with my later history and all that has been said and written about me, the situation has changed. These entries provide the only true "profile" that can be drawn. That is why, during recent years, I have reckoned with the possibility of publication, though I have continued to write for myself, not for the public.

If you find them worth publishing, you have my permission to do so—as a sort of white book *concerning my negotiations with myself—and with God.*

Dag

FOREWORD

To the symmetrical natures religion is indeed a crown
of glory; nevertheless, so far as this world is concerned, they can grow and prosper without it. But to
the unsymmetrical natures religion is a necessary condition of successful work even in this world.

LORD ACTON

A reader of *Markings* may well be surprised by what it
does *not* contain—that Dag Hammarskjöld should not
make a single direct reference to his career as an international civil servant, to the persons he met, or the
historical events of his time in which he played an important role—but if he is surprised by what it does contain, then he cannot have read the credo which, shortly
after his appointment as Secretary General, Hammarskjöld wrote for a radio program of Edward Murrow's.

From generations of soldiers and government officials
on my father's side I inherited a belief that no life was
more satisfactory than one of selfless service to your
country—or humanity. This service required a sacrifice
of all personal interests, but likewise the courage to
stand up unflinchingly for your convictions.
From scholars and clergymen on my mother's side
I inherited a belief that, in the very radical sense of

the Gospels, all men were equals as children of God, and should be met and treated by us as our masters.

Faith is a state of the mind and the soul. . . . The language of religion is a set of formulas which register a basic spiritual experience. It must not be regarded as describing in terms to be defined by philosophy, the reality which is accessible to our senses and which we can analyze with the tools of logic. I was late in understanding what this meant. When I finally reached that point, the beliefs in which I was once brought up and which, in fact, had given my life direction even while my intellect still challenged their validity, were recognized by me as mine in their own right and by my free choice . . . the explanation of how man should live a life of active social service in full harmony with himself as a member of the community of the spirit, I found in the writings of those great medieval mystics for whom "self-surrender" had been the way to self-realization, and who in "singleness of mind" and "inwardness" had found strength to say Yes to every demand which the needs of their neighbors made them face, and to say Yes also to every fate life had in store for them. . . . Love—that much misused and misinterpreted word—for them meant simply an overflowing of the strength with which they felt themselves filled when living in true self-oblivion. And this love found natural expression in an unhesitant fulfillment of duty and an unreserved acceptance of life, whatever it brought them personally of toil, suffering—or happiness.

In *Markings*, Hammarskjöld records his gradual discovery of what saying Yes to his neighbor and to Fate would mean and involve, and the various tribulations and temptations, of the Flesh, the World, and the Devil, which made this so hard for him, as they do for all of us, to say.

Had the responsibility for the decision to publish the diary been mine, I should have been inclined to omit his covering letter to Leif Belfrage on account of one sentence in it which seems to me both false and misleading.

These entries provide the only true "profile" that can be drawn.

Even if the book were as extensive and detailed a "confession" as those of Boswell or Rousseau or Gide, this statement would still be false. No man can draw his own "profile" correctly because, as Thoreau said: "It is as hard to see oneself as to look backwards without turning round." The truth is that our friends—and our enemies—always know us better than we know ourselves. There are, to be sure, a few corrective touches to their picture of us which only we can add, and these, as a rule, are concerned with our vulnerabilities and our weaknesses.

It is, for example, axiomatic that we should all think of ourselves as being more sensitive than other people because, when we are insensitive in our dealings with others, we cannot be aware of it at the time: conscious insensitivity is a self-contradiction.

Secondly, we can hardly avoid thinking that the majority of persons we meet have stronger characters than we. We cannot observe others making choices; we only know what, in fact, they do, and how, in fact, they behave. Provided their actions are not criminal, their behavior not patently vicious, and their performance of their job in life reasonably efficient, they will strike us as strong characters. But nobody can honestly think of himself as a strong character because, however successful he may be in overcoming them, he is necessarily aware of the doubts and temptations that accompany every important choice. Unless he is a crook or has made an utter mess of his life, he will recognize the truth of Cesare Pavese's observation: "We can all do good deeds, but very few of us can think good thoughts."

If we read *Markings* without remembering all the time that it was written by a man who was a great "worldly" success, we shall fail to grasp the meaning of the sadness and "unworldliness" of many of the entries. What we read here needs, for example, to be complemented by reading his public speeches—there is an excellent selection from them, made by Mr. Wilder Foote, formerly Director of Press and Publications at the U. N., and published by Harper & Row under the title *Servant of Peace* (1962)—and accounts by others of the impression Hammarskjöld made on them.

Mr. Foote, for instance, writes:

He was sustained and inspired by pure and firmly founded beliefs and ideals about life and human relationships to which he was true in word and act. To these he joined a very brilliant, orderly, pragmatic and subtle mind, capable of lightning speed in both comprehension and construction, yet strictly disciplined. He always had a firm grip on realities and he could be as disappointed by wishful thinking or shallow optimism as by cynicism or self-serving.

He was infinitely careful in the planning and execution of all he attempted, in calm acceptance and understanding of human limitations—including his own—and of the often harsh realities with which he must work. At the same time his courage was that of the medieval mystics to whom he refers in his confession of faith. . . . This, combined with his natural mental and physical endurance, carried him through 18 and 20 hour working days for weeks on end in times of crisis.

The Danish diplomat, Eyvind Bartels, in a mainly hostile review of *Markings,* testifies to Hammarskjöld's powers of foresight:

It was shortly after the war, at a meeting between the Danish Government and the Swedish, that I first saw Hammarskjöld. He was introduced by his friends in the Swedish Government as a prodigy and impressed us as such. In a long speech he discussed problems of economic policy in relation to the United States which, to us, who had lived in another more brutal world than the Swedish one, seemed pretty remote. And yet in retrospect one can see that Hammarskjöld had formulated the economic-political problems which were later to dominate the Atlantic debate.

The next time I saw him was in Paris in 1947 during the discussion of the Marshall Plan. He brushed aside Dollar Aid as of secondary importance and raised the central question, the consequence for national sovereignty of this new co-operation. At the time this seemed to us a too theoretical point of view, but, here again, one can see in retrospect that Dag Hammarskjöld had sensed a European problem which today is as burning as ever, and has not yet found its solution.

Particularly interesting, in the light of his diary, is the impression he made on a fellow student at Uppsala, P. O. Ekelöf, with whom he went on camping trips in Lapland.

His sense of duty and his industriousness did not weigh heavily on him. On the contrary, he seemed to have a happy nature. . . . Amidst all his intellectualism, sense of responsibility, and idealistic enthusiasm, there was in the young Dag Hammarskjöld something of the playful lad. (*Ergo International*, Uppsala, 1963)

My own testimony is unimportant, but I want to give it. Brief and infrequent as our meetings were, I loved the man from the moment I saw him. His knowledge and understanding of poetry, the only field in which I was competent to judge the quality of his mind, were extraordinary, and, presumptuous as it sounds, I felt certain of a mutual sympathy between us, of an unexpressed dialogue beneath our casual conversation. The loneliness and the religious concern which his diary records, I sensed; indeed, I think the only two things which, while translating it, came as a real surprise, were his familiarity with the Anglican Psalter, and his fascination with the haiku as a poetic form.

As regards the earlier entries, the question arises: "When were they written?" Before 1953 no entry is precisely dated. In the Swedish edition there are four pages dated 1925–30, five dated 1941–2, thirteen dated 1945–9, after which the entries are grouped by single years. Writing in December 1956, Hammarskjöld says:

> These notes?—They were signposts you began to set up after you had reached a point where you needed them, a fixed point that was on no account to be lost sight of.

And it is presumably this "fixed point" to which he refers in the entry for Whitsunday, 1961.

> But at some moment I did answer *Yes* to Someone—or Something—and from that hour I was certain that existence is meaningful and that, therefore, my life, in self-surrender, had a goal.

Whenever this fixed point was reached, it must have been later than the entry, dated 1952, where he says:

> What I ask for is absurd: that life shall have a meaning.
> What I strive for is impossible: that my life shall acquire a meaning.

If these three statements are to be taken literally, then one would have to conclude that the whole book was composed after the 1952 entry, and this seems highly improbable. On the other hand, however they are interpreted, it makes it difficult to believe that many of the earlier entries, in the exact form in which we have them, are contemporary with the events and experiences they describe. The most plausible guess, I should say, is that Hammarskjöld had kept some sort of a diary for a long time and that, after the crucial moment in his life when he said Yes, he went through it, cutting a lot, rewriting many entries, and, perhaps, adding some entirely new ones.

The book, for example, opens and closes with a poem, both poems depicting a *paysage moralisé*. It is hard to believe that this is a mere temporal accident. Further, in the opening poem, Hammarskjöld speaks of a man

> Ready at any moment to gather everything
> Into one simple sacrifice.

I simply cannot believe that, at the age of twenty, he thought in exactly the same terms as he was to think in thirty years later. It even seems to me doubtful whether the last entry for 1949 was written at the time.

> O Caesarea Philippi: to accept condemnation of the Way as its fulfillment, its definition, to accept this both when it is chosen and when it is realized.

Some people, no doubt, will condemn such retrospective revisions (assuming that they were made) as dishonest, but such criticisms are unjust. I am sure it is everyone's experience, as it has been mine, that any "discovery" we make about ourselves or the meaning of life is never, like a scientific discovery, a coming upon something entirely new and unsuspected: it is, rather, the coming to conscious recognition of something which we really knew all the time, but, because we were unwilling or unable to formulate it correctly, we did not hitherto know we knew. If we desire to rewrite things we wrote when we were younger, it is because we feel that they are false, and were false at the time we wrote them: what, in fact, our real experience was, we were at the time unwilling or unable to say. To all experiences, other than purely sensory ones, the maxim *credo ut intelligam* applies.

To the outward eye, Dag Hammarskjöld's career was, from the very beginning, one of uninterrupted success. He does brilliantly at college. After a short spell of teaching, he enters government service. By the age of thirty-one he has become Under-Secretary of State for Financial Affairs, and by thirty-six, Chairman of the National Bank of Sweden. In addition to the success which his talents and industry win for him, his life, to the outward eye, is exceptionally fortunate. He has never known poverty, he enjoys excellent health, and, as a citizen of a neutral country, he is spared the privations, sufferings, and horrors inflicted by the war upon the majority of people in Europe. Inwardly, however, in spite of all these advantages—in part, perhaps, because of them—there is great spiritual distress. The portrait of the up-and-coming young man that emerges from the earlier pages of *Markings* is of one of those "unsymmetric" natures which can all too easily come to grief.

An exceptionally aggressive superego—largely created, I suspect, by his relation to his father—which demands that *a* Hammarskjöld shall do and be better than other people; on the other hand, an ego weakened by a "thorn in the flesh" which convinces him that he can never hope to experience what, for most people, are the two greatest joys earthly life has to offer, either a passionate devotion returned, or a lifelong happy marriage. Consequently, a feeling of personal unworthiness which went very far, for it led him, it would seem, to undervalue or even doubt the reality of the friendship and sympathy which must always have been offered him in plenty. Consequently, too, a narcissistic fascination with himself. In two of his sharpest aphorisms, he points out that Narcissus is not the victim of vanity; his fate is that of someone who responds to his sense of unworthiness with defiance.

Further, though endowed with many brilliant gifts, not, I think, a genius, not, that is to say, a person with a single overwhelming talent and passion for some particular activity—be it poetry or physics or bird-watching—which determines, usually early in life, exactly what his function on earth is to be.

Excellent economist as he was, I do not imagine that his fellow economists would consider Hammarskjöld an original genius in this field, like Keynes, for example. Geniuses are the luckiest of mortals because what they must do is the same as what they most want to do and, even if their genius is unrecognized in their lifetime, the essential earthly reward is always theirs, the certainty that their work is good and will stand the test of time. One suspects that the geniuses will be least in the Kingdom of Heaven—if, indeed, they ever make it; they have had their reward.

To be gifted but not to know how best to make use of one's gifts, to be highly ambitious but at the same time to feel unworthy, is a dangerous combination which can often end in mental breakdown or suicide and, as the earlier entries show, the thought of suicide was not strange to Hammarskjöld. He describes two actual suicides, presumably witnessed by him personally, with fascination. When he has an automobile accident, his last thought before losing consciousness is, he tells us, a happy thought: "Well, *my* job's done."*
And, as late as 1952, he admits that suicide is a real temptation to him.

---

* I am informed that this accident must have happened to some-body else. W. H. A.

So! *that* is the way in which you are tempted to overcome your loneliness—by making the ultimate escape
from life. No! It may be that death is to be your ultimate gift to life: it must not be an act of treachery
against it.

Long before he discovered a solution, Hammarskjöld
knew exactly what his problem was—if he was not to
go under, he must learn how to forget himself and find
a calling in which he could forget himself—and knew
that it was not in his own power to do this. The
transition from despair over himself to faith in God
seems to have been a slow process, interrupted by
relapses. Two themes came to preoccupy his thoughts.
First, the conviction that no man can do properly what
he is called upon to do in this life unless he can learn
to forget his ego and act as an instrument of God. Second, that for him personally, the way to which he was
called would lead to the Cross, i.e., to suffering, worldly
humiliation, and the physical sacrifice of his life.

Both notions are, of course, highly perilous. The man
who says, "Not I, but God in me" is always in great
danger of imagining that he *is* God, and some critics
have not failed to accuse Hammarskjöld of precisely
this kind of megalomania, and to cite in evidence such
entries as the following:

If you fail, it is God, thanks to your having betrayed
Him, who will fail mankind. You fancy you can be
responsible *to* God: can you carry the responsibility
for God?

This accusation cannot be disproved by anything Hammarskjöld said or wrote, because humility and demonic
pride speak the same language.

"By their fruits," however, "you shall know them."
The man who has come to imagine he is God may be
unaware of it himself, but he very soon starts to behave

in a way which makes it obvious enough to others. One minor symptom, for example, is a refusal to listen to or tolerate the presence of others unless they say what he wishes to hear. And it is not long before he develops a paranoid suspicion of everyone else, combined with a cynical contempt for them. Had this been true of Hammarskjöld, those who worked or had dealings with him would have recorded it. But, in fact, his close colleagues in the Secretariat have all commented upon his exceptional patience in listening to what others had to say, and, even when the Russians were most bitterly attacking him over the Congo, calling him a murderer, they attacked him as an agent of imperialism, not as a self-appointed dictator, serving his personal interests.

His preoccupation with sacrifice in a literal physical sense is, maybe, a little more vulnerable. Though he was well aware of the masochistic element in his nature.

> The *arrêt* that leads to the summit separates two abysses: the pleasure-tinged death wish (not, perhaps, without an element of narcissistic masochism), and the animal fear arising from the physical instinct for survival.

I am not sure that it did not color and, to some degree, distort his thinking about the subject. "Just how," I find myself thinking, "did he envisage his end? Did he expect to be assassinated like Count Bernadotte? To be lynched by an infuriated General Assembly? Or simply to drop dead from a heart attack brought on by overwork?" As we all know, he *was* killed in the course of duty, but it is difficult to think of an airplane crash as an "act of sacrifice" in the sense in which Hammarskjöld uses the term. It could happen to any of us, regardless of any "commitment."

On the other hand, I do not think he is exaggerating in his portrayal of his life as Secretary General, despite its excitements and moments of joyous satisfaction, which he gratefully admits, as a *via crucis*. To be Secretary General of the U. N., he once jokingly told me, is like being a secular Pope, and the Papal throne is a lonely eminence. As the head of an international organization, the Secretary General cannot afford to show personal preferences for one person in it to another, for favoritism will arouse the suspicion of undue influence. As for friends in private walks of life, he simply hasn't the time to see them. In addition to the spiritual suffering of loneliness, of having to leave behind him "the world which had made him what he was," Hammarskjöld had to endure, and all the more severely because of his extreme conscientiousness, the plain physical suffering of constant nervous strain and overwork. If, as the reader goes through the entries between 1953 and 1957, he finds himself becoming impatient—and I must confess that I sometimes did—with their relentless earnestness and not infrequent repetitiousness, let him remember that most of them must have been written by a man at the extreme limits of mental and physical exhaustion. A man who has had only four or five hours sleep a night for weeks can hardly be expected to show levity or the strictest concern for stylistic niceties. Let him remember, too, that a man who, like Hammarskjöld, deliberately sets out to eliminate all selfish or self-regarding motives from his work, to act solely for the good of others and the glory of God, thereby deprives his "flesh" of the only consolations, like the prospect of money or fame, which can alleviate the pains of toil. As Simone Weil has written:

> The same suffering is much harder to bear for a high motive than for a base one. The people who stood motionless, from one to eight in the morning, for the sake of having an egg, would have found it very difficult to do in order to save a human life.

Last, I do not think that, for a man of Hammarskjöld's temperament, political life was the "natural" milieu. By training, he was a civil servant, that is to say, someone whose job it is to carry out a policy, not to decide one. He may, on the basis of his experience or convictions, advise for or against a given policy, but it is for his Minister to decide, and for him to execute that decision. This means that, though he is in public service, he does not enter the arena of public life and public controversy. Ideally, the post of Secretary General to the U. N. should be that of an international civil servant, but so long as the world is politically organized as a number of sovereign nations, often at odds with each other, it is inevitably a political post as well. On a number of occasions Hammarskjöld found himself in the position of taking a political decision, either because he was instructed to or because a deadlock between the great powers left him no option. His conception of what, in such an historical situation, should be meant by the "neutrality" of the Secretary General is best given in his own words.

He is not requested to be a neuter in the sense that he has to have no sympathies or antipathies, that there are no interests which are close to him in his personal capacity or that he is to have no ideas or ideals that matter to him. However, he is requested to be fully aware of those human reactions and meticulously to check himself so that they are not permitted to influence his actions. This is nothing unique. Is not every judge professionally under the same obligation? . . .

In the last analysis, this is a question of integrity, and if integrity in the sense of respect for law and respect for truth were to drive him into positions of conflict with this or that interest, then that conflict is a sign of his neutrality and not of his failure to observe neutrality—then it is in line, not in conflict, with his duties as an international civil servant. (*Lecture delivered to Congregation at Oxford University, May 30, 1961)*

And, of course, such conflicts arose.

The milieu of the politician is the arena of public debate, and, to feel at home in it, calls for a very tough hide indeed, invulnerable to all arrows of criticism, however sharp or venomous. One gets the impression from this book that Hammarskjöld not only failed to develop such a hide, but remained more thin-skinned than most men. He seems to have felt any criticism, no matter how obviously motivated by party or national interests, as a reflection upon his personal integrity, and this sensitivity must have made life exceptionally difficult for him when he was involved in highly controversial political issues.

It makes me very happy to see that, in the last three years of his life, he took to writing poems, for it is proof to me that he had at last acquired a serenity of mind for which he had long prayed. When a man can occupy himself with counting syllables, either he has not yet attempted any spiritual climb, or he is over the hump.

Judged by purely aesthetic standards, the entries are of varying merit. Hammarskjöld, it seems to me, was essentially an "occasional" writer; that is to say, Hammarskjöld on Hammarskjöld, his personal experiences, feelings, doubts, self-reproaches, is always interesting, but when he is making general statements about the nature of the spiritual life or the "noughting" of the self, one feels one has read it all before somewhere, in Meister Eckhart, St. John of the Cross, *The Cloud of Unknowing,* or Juliana of Norwich. He lacks the originality of insight into general problems displayed by such contemporaries as Simone Weil, for example, or Charles Williams.

Markings, however, was not intended to be read simply as a work of literature. It is also an historical document of the first importance as an account—and I cannot myself recall another—of the attempt by a professional man of action to unite in one life the *via activa* and the *via contemplativa*. Most of the famous mystics were members of one contemplative Order or another: from time to time they might give advice, bidden or unbidden, to princes temporal and spiritual, but they did not think of giving advice or taking part in the affairs of this world as their function.

There are cases of men, like Lancelot Andrewes, holding positions of high authority in the Church, who have left behind them records of their private devotions, but their life of actions was in the ecclesiastical, not the secular sphere. Certainly, both mystic monk or nun and pious bishop would be startled by Hammarskjöld's statement:

In our era, the road to holiness necessarily passes through the world of action.

As the records of the mystics show, the great temptation of the contemplative life—many of them passed through periods when they succumbed to it—is some form or other of Quietism, an indifference to and impatience with, not only "works" in the conventional sense, but also all the institutional and intellectual aspects of human life. As a professional civil servant, the head of a complex institution, and an economist, Hammarskjöld was, in his public secular life, protected from this temptation and exposed only to the usual "worldly" ones, which, because they are much easier to recognize, are less dangerous. In his personal religious life, I am not sure that he altogether escaped it. Professor Whitehead was a very wise man, but he once said a very silly thing: "Religion is what a man does with his solitude." Hammarskjöld's religion as revealed in *Markings* seems to me to be more of a solitary and private thing than it should have been. He understood very well and tried his best to practice such Gospel injunctions as "When thou doest alms, let not thy left hand know what thy right hand doeth" and "When thou fastest, anoint thy head and wash thy face, that thou appear not unto men to fast," but he does not seem to have pondered much upon such a saying as "Where two or three are gathered together in my name, I will grant their request" and he was, perhaps, a little overly impatient with doctrinal formulations: dogmatic theology may, like grammar, seem a tiresome subject, except to specialists, but, like the rules of grammar, it is a necessity. It is possible that his lack of participation in the liturgical and sacramental life of a church was a deliberate act of self-sacrifice on his part, that, as Secretary General, he felt any public commitment to a particular Christian body would label him as too "Western," but he gives no evidence in his diary of desiring such a commitment. In any case, I am sorry for his sake, because it is precisely the introverted intellectual character who stands most in need of the ecclesiastical routine, both as a discipline and as a refreshment.

But how frivolous all such misgivings look in the light of the overall impression which the book makes, the conviction when one has finished it, that one has had the privilege of being in contact with a great, good, and lovable man.

W. H. AUDEN

POSTSCRIPT

It is no secret that I do not know a single word of Swedish. When I was asked to undertake this translation, I knew I should have to refuse unless I could find as a collaborator someone who *(a)* was Swedish, *(b)* knew English well enough to give me a list of alternative words to choose among when the original Swedish word has overtones that are not exactly matchable in English, and *(c)* would be self-effacing enough to be willing to give me a literal word by word translation without trying to do my part of the job as well. In finding Mr. Leif Sjöberg, I had a fantastic stroke of good luck, and I cannot thank him enough for his unselfishness, patience, and meticulous concern for every detail. If our translation has any merit, the credit is mostly his; for any unjustifiable departure from the original, the responsibility is entirely mine.

Hammarskjöld's style is very condensed and there are places where Mr. Sjöberg confessed that the exact meaning of the Swedish baffled him. Obscurity raises a special problem for the translator. A writer bears the responsibility for what he writes. If somebody says to him, "I don't understand this passage," he can say either, "It means just what it says. But, since you seem rather stupid, I will put it in this way," or, "I'm afraid you're right. As it stands, the passage doesn't say what I meant it to say. What I should have written is as follows." In an case where the original is really obscure, that is to say, the translator's difficulty in understanding it is not due to his own ignorance or stupidity, what is he to do? Should he give as literal a translation as he can, and thus write an English sentence which he cannot himself understand, or should he write an intelligible English sentence at the cost of altering what the original text actually says? Personally, in cases of desperation, I believe he should take the second course.

The commoner difficulty in translating is, of course, the word for which no exact English equivalent exists. In *Markings*, most of such words turned out to be of German origin. I don't want to see the word *insats (Einsatz)* again for a long long time.

Another is the word or phrase for which a literal equivalent exists, but that has acquired, by historical or social accident, comic or embarrassing associations. The title of this book, *Vägmärken*, is an example. Any more or less literal translation, such as *Trail Marks* or *Guideposts*, immediately conjures up in a British or American reader an image of a Boy Scout, or of that dreadful American college phenomenon, Spiritual Emphasis Week, at which talks are given entitled *Spiritual Guideposts*.

One last point. Like most educated Swedes, Hammarskjöld was polyglottal: he frequently quotes in English, French, and German, and his Swedish publishers evidently assume that their public is well-enough acquainted with these tongues not to require a translation. I am sure that the average British or American reader would have no difficulty with the French quotations, but I am less confident about his command of German, and if one was to be translated, then it would look odd if the other were not as well. So, aside from a few isolated phrases, we have given all his quoted passages in English. If the more scholarly reader feels that he has been translated down to, we can only offer our apologies.

W. H. A.

NOTE

Since the original publication of *Markings*, scholars have attributed the original source of the words "Only the hand that erases can write the true thing" on page xxv to the Swedish poet Bertil Malmberg (1889–1958), probably inspired by Meister Eckhart.

ACKNOWLEDGMENTS

For their kindness and help in various matters, we should like to thank Mr. Leif Belfrage, Mr. Bo Beskow, Mr. Cahoon of the Morgan Library, Dean Andrew Cordier, Mr. Gunnar Ekelöf, Mr. Karl Ragnar Gierow, Mr. Per Lind, Mr. Erik Lindegren, Mrs. Elizabeth Mayer, Miss Lisa McGaw, Mr. Michael Meyer, Miss Hannah Platz, Miss Barbara Roth, Mr. Brian Urquhart, Mr. Uno Willers, Mr. Sverker Åström.

L. S.
W. H. A.

*Only the hand that erases
can write the true thing*

MEISTER ECKHART

1925-1930

THUS IT WAS

I am being driven forward
Into an unknown land.
The pass grows steeper,
The air colder and sharper.
A wind from my unknown goal
Stirs the strings
Of expectation.

Still the question:
Shall I ever get there?
There where life resounds,
A clear pure note
In the silence.

Smiling, sincere, incorruptible—
His body disciplined and limber.
A man who had become what he could,
And was what he was—
Ready at any moment to gather everything
Into one simple sacrifice.

*

Tomorrow we shall meet,
Death and I—
And he shall thrust his sword
Into one who is wide awake.

But in the meantime how grievous the memory
Of hours frittered away.

Beauty: a note that set the heartstrings quivering as it flew by; the shimmer of the blood beneath a skin translucent in the sunlight.

Beauty: the wind which refreshed the traveler, not the stifling heat in dark adits where beggars grubbed for gold.

*

Never look down to test the ground before taking your next step: only he who keeps his eye fixed on the far horizon will find his right road.

*

Life yields only to the conqueror. Never accept what can be gained by giving in. You will be living off stolen goods, and your muscles will atrophy.

*

Never measure the height of a mountain, until you have reached the top. Then you will see how low it was.

*

"Better than other people." Sometimes he says: "That, at least, you are." But more often: "Why should you be? Either you are what you can be, or you are not—like other people."

*

What you have to attempt—to be yourself. What you have to pray for—to become a mirror in which, according to the degree of purity of heart you have attained, the greatness of life will be reflected.

*

Every deed and every relationship is surrounded by an atmosphere of silence. Friendship needs no words—it is solitude delivered from the anguish of loneliness.

*

If your goal is not determined by your most secret pathos, even victory will only make you painfully aware of your own weakness.

*

Life only demands from you the strength you possess. Only one feat is possible—not to have run away.

*

To be sure, you have to fence with an unbuttoned foil: but, in the loneliness of yesterday, did you not toy with the idea of poisoning the tip?

*

We carry our nemesis within us: yesterday's self-admiration is the legitimate father of today's feeling of guilt.

*

He bore failure without self-pity, and success without self-admiration. Provided he knew he had paid his uttermost farthing, what did it matter to him how others judged the result.

A Pharisee? Lord, thou knowest he has never been righteous in his own eyes.

1941-1942

THE MIDDLE YEARS

He stood erect—as a peg top does so long as the whip keeps lashing it. He was modest—thanks to a robust conviction of his own superiority. He was unambitious —all he wanted was a life free from cares, and he took more pleasure in the failures of others than in his own successes. He saved his life by never risking it—and complained that he was misunderstood.

*

"The Army of Misfortune." Why should we always think of this as meaning "The Others"?

*

Your cravings as a human animal do not become a prayer just because it is God whom you ask to attend to them.

*

Isn't the void which surrounds you when the noise ceases your just reward for a day devoted to preventing others from neglecting you?

*

What gives life its value you can find—and lose. But never possess. This holds good above all for "the Truth about Life."

*

How can you expect to keep your powers of hearing when you never want to listen? That God should have time for you, you seem to take as much for granted as that you cannot have time for Him.

*

The devils enter uninvited when the house stands empty. For other kinds of guests, you have first to open the door.

*

"Upon my conditions."* To live under that sign is to purchase knowledge about the Way at the price of loneliness.

*

There is only one path out of the steamy dense jungle where the battle is fought over glory and power and advantage—one escape from the snares and obstacles you yourself have set up. And that is—to accept death.

*

---

* A quotation from Vilhelm Ekelund, a Swedish aphorist, who had a considerable influence on H. W. H. A.

The more faithfully you listen to the voice within you, the better you will hear what is sounding outside. And only he who listens can speak. Is this the starting point of the road towards the union of your two dreams—to be allowed in clarity of mind to mirror life and in purity of heart to mold it?

*

Openness to life grants a lightning-swift insight into the life situation of others. What is necessary?—to wrestle with your problem until its emotional discomfort is clearly conceived in an intellectual form—and then act accordingly.

*

It makes one's heart ache when one sees that a man has staked his soul upon some end, the hopeless imperfection and futility of which is immediately obvious to everyone but himself. But isn't this, after all, merely a matter of degree? Isn't the pathetic grandeur of human existence in some way bound up with the eternal disproportion in this world, where self-delusion is necessary to life, between the honesty of the striving and the nullity of the result? That we all—every one of us—take ourselves seriously is not *merely* ridiculous.

*

He tends a garden, the borders of which have, without his knowledge, been set by his own powers. His pride in tending it well and his blindness to everything that lies outside its borders make him a little self-opinionated. But is this any worse than the slightly irritable contempt of the man who cannot so deceive himself and has therefore chosen to fight *extra muros?*

*

". . . and have not charity." Isn't the fulfillment of our duty towards our neighbor an expression of our deepest desire? It very well may be. In any case, why torture ourselves in order to hurt others?

*

Praise nauseates you—but woe betide him who does not recognize your worth.

*

The Strait Road—to live for others in order to save one's soul. The Broad—to live for others in order to save one's self-esteem.

*

So! We are to believe that misfortune is the fault of those it strikes—a fault which sooner or later will blossom into crime, unless the unfortunate one keeps silent about his fate.

*

You cannot play with the animal in you without becoming wholly animal, play with falsehood without forfeiting your right to truth, play with cruelty without losing your sensitivity of mind. He who wants to keep his garden tidy doesn't reserve a plot for weeds.

*

If you don't speak ill of others more often than you do, this certainly isn't from any lack of desire. But you know that malice only gives you elbowroom when dispensed in carefully measured doses.

*

9

You are your own god—and are surprised when you find that the wolf pack is hunting you across the desolate ice fields of winter.

*

"Hallowed be Thy Name." When all your strength ought to be focused into one pencil of light pointing up through the darkness, you allow it to be dissipated in a moss fire where nothing is consumed, but *all* life is suffocated.

*

When all becomes silent around you, and you recoil in terror—see that your work has become a flight from suffering and responsibility, your unselfishness a thinly disguised masochism; hear, throbbing within you, the spiteful, cruel heart of the steppe wolf—do not then anesthetize yourself by once again calling up the shouts and horns of the hunt, but gaze steadfastly at the vision until you have plumbed its depths.

*

On the bookshelf of life, God is a useful work of reference, always at hand but seldom consulted. In the whitewashed hour of birth, He is a jubilation and a refreshing wind, too immediate for memory to catch. But when we are compelled to look ourselves in the face—then He rises above us in terrifying reality, beyond all argument and "feeling," stronger than all self-defensive forgetfulness.

*

The road to self-knowledge does not pass through faith. But only through the self-knowledge we gain by pursuing the fleeting light in the depth of our being do we reach the point where we can grasp what faith is. How many have been driven into outer darkness by empty talk about faith as something to be rationally comprehended, something "true."

*

Our secret creative will divines its counterpart in others, experiencing its own universality, and this intuition builds a road towards knowledge of the power which is itself a spark within us.

1945-1949

TOWARDS NEW SHORES———?

At every moment you choose yourself. But do you choose *your* self? Body and soul contain a thousand possibilities out of which you can build many *I*'s. But in only one of them is there a congruence of the elector and the elected. Only one—which you will never find until you have excluded all those superficial and fleeting possibilities of being and doing with which you toy, out of curiosity or wonder or greed, and which hinder you from casting anchor in the experience of the mystery of life, and the consciousness of the talent entrusted to you which is your *I*.

Soaked, dark, woollen garments. Deprecating glances.
Tired mouths. It is late.

The business proceeds with indifference and dispatch.
At the polished black marble tombstone of the counter,
many are still waiting.

A sexless light from white ramps is reflected in glass
and enamel. Outside stands the darkness. The street
door bangs and a wave of raw dampness breaks in
upon the dry air, saturated with chemicals.

"O Life, thou embracing, warm, rich, blessed word!"
(Verner von Heidenstam)

Then he looks up from behind the scales on one of the
high desks—wise, good-natured, withdrawn in concen-
tration. Deep wrinkles in a gray skin bear witness to a
gentle irony, born of experience and a long life within
four walls.

> Here and now—only this is real:
> The good face of an old man,
> Caught naked in an unguarded moment,
> Without past, without future.

She knew that nothing would get better, that it would never be any different. He had lost interest in his work, and no longer did anything. Because, he said, he was not given a free hand. And now she was sitting there praying for his freedom, praying because she so wanted to believe that he was being unfairly treated, that, if only he was given his freedom, he would become a man again. Wanted to believe it so that she might keep up her belief in him. She knew what the true answer was, but she had to force herself to listen to it: he was as free as anybody can be in the economic mazes of a modern society, and any external change would only bring him fresh disappointment. The situation would repeat itself, and he would discover that everything was just as it had been before.

Yes, yes— And she knew more: knew that there could never be a way out. Because behind all his talk of freedom lay hidden a child's wish to conquer death, a lack of interest in any piece of work the result of which would not be *his,* even long after he was dead. —And yet she sat there praying.

Before it became clear to us what had happened, he was already too far out. We could do nothing. We only saw how the undertow was dragging him faster and faster away from the shore. Saw his futile and exhausting struggle to touch the bottom beneath his feet.

It was only blind instinct which drove him to try and save his life: in his mind he had cut himself off from reality. When, in spite of this, a flash of knowledge as to his situation forced itself upon him, he told himself that the rest of us were even worse off. And then we still took the whole matter so lightly! He would certainly still be clutching this conviction at the last moment when the gurgling whirlpool sucked him down.

It had always been this way. Dependent like a child upon admiring affection, he had always taken uncritical friendship for granted, even with those who were indifferent or actually hostile. He had always acted upon this assumption—yet, in an unconscious effort to create friendships which perhaps did not exist, not without a certain compliance towards the interests of others, and, at the same time, a fear of a collision with reality which might rend asunder his web of illusions. When things he had said were quoted against him, he denied having ever said them. And when this denial was called by its right name, he interpreted this as a symptom of his

15

critic's lack of mental balance: as time went on, psychosis became an ever commoner word on his lips.

Just what was it we felt when, for the first time, we realized that he had gone too far out ever to be able to get back?

What is one to do on a bleak day but drift for a while through the streets—drift with the stream?

Slowly, with the gravity of an inanimate object, now coming to a standstill, now turning, where currents meet, in listless leisurely gyrations. Slow—and gray. The November day has reached the hour when the light is dying behind a low cold bank of cloud, but the twilight brings no promise of mitigation or peace.

Slow and gray— He searches every face. But the people aimlessly streaming along the gray ditches of the streets are all like himself—atoms in whom the radioactivity is extinct, and force has tied its endless chain around nothing.

"That one may be translated into light and song." *(Erik Blomberg)* To let go of the image which, in the eyes of this world, bears your name, the image fashioned in your consciousness by social ambition and sheer force of will. To let go and fall, fall—in trust and blind devotion. Towards another, another. . . .

To take the risk—

In the dim light he searches every face, but sees only endless variations on his own meanness. So might Dante have imagined the punishment of those who had never taken the risk. —To reach perfection, we must all pass, one by one, through the death of self-effacement. And, on this side of it, he will never find the way to anyone who has passed through it.

17

It was probably a little too early for the snake's-head fritillaries. But the May sky shone high above the plain. The sunlight and the caroling of larks were blended into one cool ecstasy. The thaw had come, and the clay-brown water of the river was swift and fresh.

Out in the main channel, a dark bundle turns slowly. A glimpse of a face, a cry. Of its own volition, again and again it thrusts the face under the surface.

No cloud passed over the sun. The song of the lark did not stop. But the water is suddenly dirty and cold— the thought of being dragged down to the bottom by the heavy thing which is fighting out there for its death arouses a feeling of sheer nausea. And this nausea is more paralyzing than the fear of danger. Cowardice? In any case, the word must be spoken.

She walked to the end of the esplanade, and then waded out through the mud until the water was deep enough and the current swept her away. But she did not sink. The water pushed her back. Again and again, until her strength was exhausted, she opened her mouth and thrust her face under the surface. This time it must not fail. She heard cries from the bank. If they would . . .

During their attempts at artificial respiration, they have laid bare the upper part of her body. As she lies stretched out on the riverbank—beyond all human nakedness in the inaccessible solitude of death—her white firm breasts are lifted to the sunlight—a heroic torso of marble-blonde stone in the soft grass.

18

When the gun went off, he fell on his side beneath the maple trees.

The air is motionless in the moist dusk of the late July day, a dusk intensified by the heavy shadows of the leaves. His head rests in profile, the features finely chiseled but still immature—white against the gray of the sand, with a small wound in the temple. In this dead light, only the dark blood slowly welling from the nostrils has color.

Why—? Above the spreading pool of blood no questions reach the land you have sought. And no words can any longer call you back. —That eternal "Beyond" —where you are separated from us by a death chosen long before the bullet hit the temple.

It must have been late in September. Or, perhaps, my memory has invented an appropriate weather for the occasion.

"We brothers and sisters were so happy at home. I remember the Christmases when we all gathered. Who could then have believed that life would ever become so torn asunder—"

Now the words and the subdued voice come back to me—thirty years later—as her daughter writes the same epitaph upon her childhood and her life.

Descending into the valley, at the last curve he lost control of the car. As it toppled over the bank at the side of the road, his only thought was: "Well, at least my job's done."

His one, weary, happy thought.

It wasn't so: he was to go on living. But not to go on with *this* journey. When he came to, and the solid world again took shape around him, he could hardly keep back his tears—tears of self-pity and disappointment because his vacation plans had been ruined.

The one reaction was no less genuine than the other. We may be willing to turn our backs on life, but we still complain like children when life does not grant our wishes.

He was impossible. It wasn't that he didn't attend to his work: on the contrary, he took endless pains over the tasks he was given. But his manner of behavior brought him into conflict with everybody and, in the end, began to have an adverse effect on everything he had to do with.

When the crisis came and the whole truth had to come out, he laid the blame on us: in his conduct there was nothing, absolutely nothing to reproach. His self-esteem was so strongly bound up, apparently, with the idea of his innocence, that one felt a brute as one demonstrated, step by step, the contradictions in his defense and, bit by bit, stripped him naked before his own eyes. But justice to others demanded it.

When the last rag of a lie had been taken from him and we felt there was nothing more to be said, out it came with stifled sobs.

"But why did you never help me, why didn't you tell me what to do? You knew that I always felt you were against me. And fear and insecurity drove me further and further along the course you now condemn me for having taken. It's been so hard—everything. One day, I remember, I was so happy: one of you said that something I had produced was quite good—"

So, in the end, we were, in fact, to blame. We had not voiced our criticisms, but we had allowed them to stop us from giving him a single word of acknowledgment, and in this way had barred every road to improvement.

For it is always the stronger one who is to blame. We lack life's patience. Instinctively, we try to eliminate a person from our sphere of responsibility as soon as the outcome of this particular experiment by Life appears, in our eyes, to be a failure. But Life pursues her experiments far beyond the limitations of our judgment. This is also the reason why, at times, it seems so much more difficult to live than to die.

He stands alone in the mist upon the wet black stone, his rump fat and heavy, feathers padding the rounded curves of his body and the rippling reptilian muscles of his neck. Shameless amber eyes with no expression in them but that of naked voracity. A yellow, powerful beak, created for prey but without the predator's lean cruel elegance.

I have watched them floating with the tide and fighting over scraps of decaying food. Watched them making their rounds and examining the condoms which, after the weekend, have been driven into the backwater by the piers. I recall watching them on days in Autumn as they rocked ponderously in the heavy clay furrows— ungainly gatherers of worms from those gaping wounds in the soil, their sides glistening oily and slippery in the wet.

How remote it seems:
    In the last dark hour of the night, the shrill shrieks of sea gulls tear asunder the thin, skin-soft film of silence. Their cries are interwoven with their swift white gambols over the swell, the salt tang, and the awakening breeze.

His sleep had been light—like that of a wild animal. And in his sleep his senses had reached out towards the new day—

Only when I get quite close does he impel himself a few yards to one side with an indolent flap of his wings—a well-nourished carrion bird who feels so much at home among us all.

Peace—as when long bitterness has been dissolved by tears: the ground bare. Glitter of wide waters in the soft light—

Around me the soft walls of the thaw haze. The cloud ceiling is low, an orange shimmer in the setting winter sun.

In the mirror-world of the water, pale olive against pewter, the bare branches of an alder tree flap slowly, as in a gentle breeze, to the imperceptible movement of the waves.

And then:

In the soft darkness the lonely flame surrounded by a womb of warm light. The hyacinth, a white cloud above the deep well of gloom in the mirror, barely glimpsed, glittering through the whispering forest of books.

Not for us now, perhaps never for us:

In the silence the ring of the telephone forever subtracts the conversation we have run away from but never shall escape.

Beneath the hush a whisper from long ago, promising peace of mind and a burden shared.

No peace which is not peace for all, no rest until all has been fulfilled.

He seeks his own comfort—
and is rewarded with glimpses of satisfaction followed by a long period of emptiness and shame
which sucks him dry.
He fights for his position—
all his talk about the necessary preconditions for
doing something worthwhile prove an insecure
barrier against self-disgust.
He devotes himself to his job—
but he is in doubt as to its importance and, therefore, constantly looking for recognition: perhaps
he is slowly nearing the point where he will feel
grateful when he is not criticized, but he is still a
very long way from accepting criticism when he is.

You asked for burdens to carry— And howled when
they were placed on your shoulders. Had you fancied
another sort of burden? Did you believe in the anonym-
ity of sacrifice? The sacrificial act and the sacrificial
victim are opposites, and to be judged as such.

O Caesarea Philippi:* to accept condemnation of
the Way as its fulfillment, its definition, to accept this
both when it is chosen and when it is realized.

---

* See Matthew 16:13–28. Particularly relevant, perhaps, are verses
24–25: "If any man will come after me, let him deny himself, and
take up his cross, and follow me. For whosoever will save his life
shall lose it: and whosoever will lose his life for my sake shall find
it." W. H. A.

1950

—::—::—::—::—

Night is drawing nigh*——

"—and then what will all earthly joys be, compared to the promise: Where I am, there ye may be also."

In a whirling fire of annihilation,
In the storm of destruction
And deadly cold of the act of sacrifice,
You would welcome death.
But when it slowly grows within you,
Day by day,
You suffer anguish
Anguish under the unspoken judgment which hangs over
 your life,
While leaves fall in the fool's paradise.
The chooser's happiness lies in his congruence with the
 chosen,

---

* The Swedish original, *Snart stundar natten*—literally, *Soon the night is at hand*—is taken from a hymn by Bishop Franzén which H.'s mother used always to read aloud on New Year's Eve. I have used a line by Baring-Gould because it has the same meaning and his hymn *Now the day is over* is as familiar to English readers as Bishop Franzén's is to the Swedish. W. H. A.

The peace of iron filings, obedient to the forces of the
    magnetic field—
Calm is the soul that is emptied of all self,
In a restful harmony—
This happiness is here and now,
In the eternal moment of co-inherence.
A happiness within you—but not yours.

The anguish of loneliness brings blasts from the storm
center of death: only that can be really yours which is
another's, for only what you have given, be it only in
the gratitude of acceptance, is salvaged from the nothing
which some day will have been your life.

Sailing with the paravanes of a disingenuous affability always in position, he imagined that, in spite of his lack of skill as a navigator, he was safe from the danger of mines.

*

The lap dog disguised himself as a lamb, but tried to hunt with the wolves.

*

Out of laziness, ignorance, consciousness of an audience (were it only your own reflection in the mirror)—out of such reasons I have seen you take a risk or assume a responsibility.

*

A blown egg floats well, and sails well on every puff of wind—light enough for such performances, since it has become nothing but shell, with neither embryo nor nourishment for its growth. "A good mixer."

Without reserve or respect for privacy, anxious to please—speech without form, words without weight. Mere shells.

*

He is one of those who has had the wilderness for a pillow, and called a star his brother. Alone. But loneliness can be a communion.

*

A heart pulsating in harmony with the circulation of sap and the flow of rivers? A body with the rhythms of the earth in its movements? No. Instead: a mind, shut off from the oxygen of alert senses, that has wasted itself on "treasons, stratagems and spoils"—of importance only within four walls. A tame animal—in whom the strength of the species has outspent itself, to no purpose.

*

The overtones are lost, and what is left are conversations which, in their poverty, cannot hide the lack of real contact. We glide past each other. But why? Why—?

We reach out towards the other. In vain—because we have never dared to give ourselves.

*

An upright carriage, a symptom of health, is something very different from the hard carapace inside which, in our vacillation, we seek shelter.*

*

A modest wish: that our doings and dealings may be of a little more significance to life than a man's dinner jacket is to his digestion. Yet not a little of what we describe as our achievement is, in fact, no more than a garment in which, on festive occasions, we seek to hide our nakedness.

*

---

* Again the thought is derived from Ekelund. W. H. A.

You find it hard to forgive those who, early in life, have come to enjoy the advantages which go with maturity. Aside from any other consideration, why don't you put into the balance the long spring enjoyed by a youth who matured late?

*

Having breathed an atmosphere filled with the products of his own spiritual combustion, he remembers reading somewhere that, in the neighborhood of a sulphur works, even a sparse vegetation can only survive if it is sheltered from the wind. —"When did this happen?" he asks himself—"and through how many generations will the effects still be traceable?"

*

At any rate, your contempt for your fellow human beings does not prevent you, with a well-guarded self-respect, from trying to win their respect.

*

Time goes by: reputation increases, ability declines.

*

Giving and receiving sympathy: his kindness is undoubtedly genuine in so far as it is a symptom of a congenital tendency to fill his life with the contents of other people's.

*

Perhaps a great love is never returned. Had it been given warmth and shelter by its counterpart in the Other, perhaps it would have been hindered from ever growing to maturity.

It "gives" us nothing. But in its world of loneliness it leads us up to summits with wide vistas—of insight.

*

32

When he told me that he had many friends, could easily make new ones and have a high old time with them, it struck hard like a blow which had been very carefully aimed. A question had become meaningless.

I only understood much later, understood that his words had hurt so because my love had still a long way to go before it would mature into—love. Understood that he had reacted instinctively and justifiably in self-defense, and with a sure sense of what was the right path for me and for him.

*

A line, a shade, a color—their fiery expressiveness.

The language of flowers, mountains, shores, human bodies: the interplay of light and shade in a look, the aching beauty of a neckline, the grail of the white crocus on the alpine meadow in the morning sunshine —words in a transcendental language of the senses.

*

"Ego-love" contains an element of gourmandise which our language lacks the right cadences to express: *Mon chèr moi—âme et corps—tu me fais un grand plaisir!*

Your ego-love doesn't bloom unless it is sheltered. The rules are simple: don't commit yourself to anyone and, therefore, don't allow anyone to come close to you. Simple—and fateful. Its efforts to shelter its love create a ring of cold around the Ego which slowly eats its way inwards towards the core.

*

What a farce—your farce, O masters of men! The master of the hounds knows that he is king for but a single day in a kingdom of fools. And he knows there are better ways of dealing with a fox than the one he represents. While, on the other hand. . . .

*

On whatever social level the intrigues are begun and the battle fought, and whatever, in other respects, the external circumstances may be, when what is at stake is his own position, even the "best head" unfailingly exhibits his naïveté. The possible tricks are so few. He who pursues such a course becomes as blind and deaf as the cock capercailzie courting his hen in a fir tree— especially at those moments when he imagines he is being most astute. A grace to pray for—that our self-interest, which is inescapable, shall never cripple our sense of humor, that fully conscious self-scrutiny which alone can save us.

*

Only tell others what is of importance to them. Only ask them what you need to know. In both cases, that is, limit the conversation to what the speaker really possesses. —Argue only in order to reach a conclusion. Think aloud only with those to whom this means something. Don't let small talk fill up the time and the silence except as a medium for bearing unexpressed messages between two people who are attuned to each other. A dietary for those who have learned by experience the truth of the saying, "For every idle word. . . ." But hardly popular in social life.

*

Why this desire in all of us that, after we have disappeared, the thoughts of the living shall now and again dwell upon our name? Our *name*. Anonymous immortality we cannot even escape. The consequences of our lives and actions can no more be erased than they can be identified and duly labeled—to our honor or our shame. "The poor ye have always with you." The dead, too.

*

All men are alike—true in that the difference between those who received many talents and those who received few is presently erased without mercy. But untrue when it is a question of how they employed them: then, there still stands the frontier between life and death, as it has been drawn for all eternity. In the last analysis, however, true there also, because we are, all of us, at all times, confronted with the possibility of taking the step across that frontier—in either direction.

*

Let everything be consumed by the fire in the hope that something of value may be left which can be riddled out of the ashes.

*

Our incurable instinct to *acquire*—to assimilate in the crudest sense of the word—provides the medium for much of our aesthetic experience. Like the mountain troll* who wants to eat the princess over and over again—only over again to have the experience of being just a mountain troll. We pick the flower. We press body against body—bringing to nought that human beauty which is only physical in that the surfaces of the body are animated by a spirit inaccessible to physical touch.

*

When the conflicting currents of the unconscious create engulfing whirlpools, the waters can again be guided into a single current if the dam sluice be opened into the channel of prayer—and if that channel has been dug deep enough.

*

---

* Probably a reference to a poem by Gustav Fröding. W. H. A.

Take warning from all those times when, on meeting again, we feel ashamed because we realize we had accepted the false simplification which absence permits, its obliteration of all those characteristics which, when we meet face to face, force themselves upon even the blindest. Where human beings are concerned, the statement "nothing is true" is true—at a distance; and the converse is also true—at the moment of confrontation.

*

I observe her, behind the window across the street, playing patience, day after day, evening after evening. Patience, patience! Probably, death will not keep you waiting much longer now.

*

Jabbering away about this or that, slouching along the bypaths of gossip, unjust to himself and to others. The great thing is to charm—in order to possess, at least for the moment, a person whose feelings he doesn't dare to test by revealing his own. Better, though, this humiliating role of the clown than to be shunned as a bore—or as contemptible because of an infatuation which meets with no response.

*

The feeling of shame over the previous day when consciousness again emerges from the ocean of the night. How dreadful must the contrast have been between the daily life and the living waters to make the verdict one of high treason. It is not the repeated mistakes, the long succession of petty betrayals—though, God knows, they would give cause enough for anxiety and self-contempt —but the huge elementary mistake, the betrayal of that within me which is greater than I—in a complacent adjustment to alien demands.

*

Between experiencing and having experienced—the moment when the experience yields its last secrets. A moment we only discover is already past when cracks and stains appear, the gilding flakes off, and we wonder what it was that once so attracted us.

*

In spite of everything, your bitterness because others are enjoying what you are denied is always ready to flare up. At best it may lie dormant for a couple of sunny days. Yet, even at this unspeakably shabby level, it is still an expression of the real bitterness of death—the fact that others are allowed to go on living.

*

Like the bee, we distill poison from honey for our self-defense—what happens to the bee if it uses its sting is well known.

*

Do you really have "feelings" any longer for anybody or anything except yourself—or even that? Without the strength of a personal commitment, your experience of others is at most aesthetic.

Yet, today, even such a maimed experience brought you into touch with a portion of spiritual reality which revealed your utter poverty.

*

What must come to pass, should come to pass. Within the limits of that *must*, therefore, you are invulnerable.

He who works for his daily bread.
He who attaches importance to position.
He who enjoys his rights.
He for whom problems have ceased to exist—as he
    rests on his laurels.
And you yourself?

At the head of the narrow adit, lit only by the searchlight of the mechanical shovel which bites through the rock like the jaws of a caterpillar. Continual darkness. The same continual cold, dripping with moisture. The same continual loneliness—hemmed in by walls of rock, but without the safety of a wall.

So, out of the earth, he dug an ore which was useful and provided money. Money, some of which would go to the other three, and some to yourself.*

At least be certain in the marrow of your bones that it is not for the egotistical satisfaction of perfection in your job, but for him that you work, that what he has

---

* Evidently H. is thinking of his father, Hjalmar Hammarskjöld (1862–1953), who was Prime Minister of Sweden from 1914 to 1917 and, later, Governor of the Province of Uppland. A conservative, he was frequently accused of being a reactionary. See in the series *From Uppsala*, the haiku beginning *A box on the ear taught the boy*. See also H.'s Inaugural Address to the Swedish Academy on December 20, 1954, when he was elected to the seat left vacant by his father's death. A translation appears in *Servant of Peace*, pp. 63–79. W. H. A.

a right to demand from you takes precedence over what you have a right to demand from him.

Atonement for the guilt you carry because of your good fortune: without pity for yourself or others, to give all you are, and thus justify, at least morally, what you possess, knowing that you only have a right to demand anything of others so long as you follow this course.

Echoing silence
Darkness lit up by beams
Light
Seeking its counterpart
In melody
Stillness
Striving for liberation
In a word
Life
In dust
In shadow
How seldom growth and blossom
How seldom fruit

These wretched attempts to make an experience apprehensible (for my sake? for others?)—the tasks of the morrow—Y's friendship or X's appreciation of what I have done: paper screens which I place between myself and the void to prevent my gaze from losing itself in the infinity of time and space.

Small paper screens. Blown to shreds by the first puff of wind, catching fire from the tiniest spark. Lovingly looked after—but frequently changed.

This dizziness in the face of *les espaces infinis*—only overcome if we dare to gaze into them without any protection. And accept them as the reality before which we must justify our existence. For this is the truth we must reach to live, that everything *is* and we just in it.

Time's flight. Our flight in time—flight from
    time.
Flying on strong wings—with time,
Never lingering, never anticipating:
A rest in the movement—our victory over
    movement.
Lightly, lightly—
Soaring above the dread of the waters,
In the moment of dedication,
All strength gathered, all life at stake,
Plunging into the deep.
But no rest on the waves, constrained by
    currents.
Again over the waters, stillness over the
    swell,
Borne by the wind with the strength of our
    own wings.
Never land, never nesting place—
Until the final plunge
When the deep takes back its own.

Hunger is my native place in the land of the passions. Hunger for fellowship, hunger for righteousness—for a fellowship founded on righteousness, and a righteousness attained in fellowship.

Only life can satisfy the demands of life. And this hunger of mine can be satisfied for the simple reason that the nature of life is such that I can realize my individuality by becoming a bridge for others, a stone in the temple of righteousness.

Don't be afraid of yourself, live your individuality to the full—but for the good of others. Don't copy others in order to buy fellowship, or make convention your law instead of living the righteousness.

To become free and responsible. For this alone was man created, and he who fails to take the Way which could have been his shall be lost eternally.

＊

I am reading about some persons, long dead. Surreptitiously, other names insert themselves into the text, and, presently, I am reading about us, as *we* shall be when we are the past. Most has utterly vanished. Problems which were once so vital, spread themselves over the pages as cold abstractions—simple ones, but we failed to understand them. We appear as rather stupid, foolish, self-seeking puppets, moved by obvious strings, which, now and again, get tangled up.

It is no caricature that I encounter in the distorting mirror of historical research. Simply the proof that it has all been vanity.

At least he knew this much about himself—I know what man is—his vulgarity, lust, pride, envy—and longing.

Longing—among other things, for the Cross.

*

Is life so wretched? Isn't it rather your hands which are too small, your vision which is muddied? You are the one who must grow up.

*

We are not permitted to choose the frame of our destiny. But what we put into it is ours. He who wills adventure will experience it—according to the measure of his courage. He who wills sacrifice will be sacrificed—according to the measure of his purity of heart.

*

Never let success hide its emptiness from you, achievement its nothingness, toil its desolation. And so keep alive the incentive to push on further, that pain in the soul which drives us beyond ourselves.

Whither? That I don't know. That I don't ask to know.

*

The little urchin makes a couple of feeble hops on one leg without falling down. And is filled with admiration at his dexterity, doubly so, because there are onlookers. Do we ever grow up?

*

O how much self-discipline, nobility of soul, lofty sentiments, we can treat ourselves to, when we are well-off and everything we touch prospers— Cheap: scarcely better than believing success is the reward of virtue.

*

The dust settles heavily, the air becomes stale, the light dim in the room which we are not prepared to leave at any moment.

Our love becomes impoverished if we lack the courage to sacrifice its object.

Our will to live only survives so long as we will life without a thought as to whether it is our own or not.

*

God does not die on the day when we cease to believe in a personal deity, but we die on the day when our lives cease to be illumined by the steady radiance, renewed daily, of a wonder, the source of which is beyond all reason.

*

"Treat others as ends, never as means." And myself as an end only in my capacity as a means: to shift the dividing line in my being between subject and object to a position where the subject, even if it is in me, is outside and above me—so that my *whole* being may become an instrument for that which is greater than I.

*

It is *now,* in this very moment, that I can and must pay for all that I have received. The past and its load of debt are balanced against the present. And on the future I have no claim.

Is not beauty created at every encounter between a man and life, in which he repays his debt by focusing on the living moment all the power which life has given him as an obligation? Beauty—for the one who pays his debt. For others, too, perhaps.

The longest journey
Is the journey inwards.
Of him who has chosen his destiny,
Who has started upon his quest
For the source of his being
(Is there a source?).
He is still with you,
But without relation,
Isolated in your feeling
Like one condemned to death
Or one whom imminent farewell
Prematurely dedicates
To the loneliness which is the final lot of all.

Between you and him is distance,
Uncertainty—
Care.

He will see you withdrawing,
Further and further,
Hear your voices fading,
Fainter and fainter.

When the evening of being together was over, a feeling of emptiness bordering on guilt brought on the anguish which inevitably accompanies sloth and inadequacy.

The evening had not only been meaningless; it had been unnecessary. Staged for reasons which, in a human relation of such an ordinary character, were a surrender to the mortal sin of sloth. The comedy had to be played out to the end, filled up, as, in the circumstances, was only to be expected, with an idle chatter which degraded the living reality.

*

How undisguised your thick-skinned self-satisfied loneliness appeared before his naked agony as he struggled to make a living contact. How difficult you found it to help, when confronted in another by your own problem —uncorrupted.

*

Suddenly I saw he was more real to himself than I am to myself, and that what was required of me was to experience this reality of his not as an object but as a subject—and *more* real than mine.

1951

"Night is drawing nigh—" So! another year it is. And if this day should be your last:

"—How can we ever be the sold short or the cheated, we who for every service have long ago been overpaid?" *(Meister Eckhart)*

The pulley of time drags us inexorably forward towards this last day. A relief to think of this, to consider that there is a moment without a beyond. I can test everything between the finger and thumb of the chooser, everything—except this. When days and years are fused into a single moment, its every aspect illumined by the light of death, measurable only by the measure of death.

＊

Before an important decision someone clutches your hand—a glimpse of gold in the iron-gray, the proof of all you have never dared to believe.

＊

Time always seems long to the child who is waiting—
for Christmas, for next summer, for becoming a grown-
up: long also when he surrenders his whole soul to
each moment of a happy day. Then—

*

Out of loyalty to others he was compelled to be aggressive by *their* feelings of inferiority.

*

"Finding content in the indifference of others." And at
the same time hungering for sympathy!

*

The present moment is significant, not as the bridge between past and future, but by reason of its contents,
contents which can fill our emptiness and become ours,
if we are capable of receiving them.

"Old men ought to be explorers." *(T. S. Eliot)* Some
have to be—because the frontiers of the familiar are
closed to them. But few succeed in opening up new
lands.

*

Narcissus leant over the spring, enthralled by the only
man in whose eyes he had ever dared—or been given
the chance—to forget himself.

   Narcissus leant over the spring, enchanted by his
own ugliness, which he prided himself upon having the
courage to admit.

*

The ride on the Witches' Sabbath to the Dark Tower
where we meet only ourselves, ourselves, ourselves.

*

We cannot afford to forget any experience, not even the most painful.

*

We remember our dead. When they were born, when they passed away—either as men of promise, or as men of achievement.

*

To be "sociable"—to talk merely because convention forbids silence, to rub against one another in order to create the illusion of intimacy and contact: what an example of *la condition humaine*. Exhausting, naturally, like any improper use of our spiritual resources. In miniature, one of the many ways in which mankind successfully acts as its own scourge—in the hell of spiritual death.

*

"Lack of character—" All too easily we confuse a fear of standing up for our beliefs, a tendency to be more influenced by the convictions of others than by our own, or simply a lack of conviction—with the need that the strong and mature feel to give full weight to the arguments of the other side. A game of hide-and-seek: when the Devil wishes to play on our lack of character, he calls it tolerance, and when he wants to stifle our first attempts to learn tolerance, he calls it lack of character.

*

The aura of victory that surrounds a man of good will, the sweetness of soul which emanates from him—a flavor of cranberries and cloudberries, a touch of frost and fiery skies.

*

The shamelessness of great pride: it lifts the crown from the cushion and places it upon its brow with its own hands.*

The alienation of great pride from everything which constitutes human order.

A fable: once upon a time, there was a crown so heavy that it could only be worn by one who remained completely oblivious to its glitter.

*

Your fancy dress, the mask you put on with such care so as to appear to your best advantage was the wall between you and the sympathy you sought. A sympathy you won on the day when you stood there naked.

The voice which gave orders was only obeyed when it became a helpless wail.

*

Committed to the future—
Even if that only means *"se preparer à bien mourir."*

*

Only he deserves power who every day justifies it.

*

Mixed motives. In any crucial decision, every side of our character plays an important part, the base as well as the noble. Which side cheats the other when they stand united behind us in an action?

When, later, Mephisto appears and smilingly declares himself the winner, he can still be defeated by the manner in which we accept the consequences of our action.

*

* At his coronation Charles XII set the crown on his own head. W. H. A.

"People expected to see him emerge as a leader." He—? whose courage and character are such that he lets himself be driven, like Captain Ahab, over the oceans of his fleeing goal.

*

He was a member of the crew on Columbus's caravel— he kept wondering whether he would get back to his home village in time to succeed the old shoemaker before anybody else could grab the job.

*

There is a point at which everything becomes simple and there is no longer any question of choice, because all you have staked will be lost if you look back. Life's point of no return.

*

Around a man who has been pushed into the limelight, a legend begins to grow as it does around a dead man. But a dead man is in no danger of yielding to the temptation to nourish his legend, or accept its picture as reality. I pity the man who falls in love with his image as it is drawn by public opinion during the honeymoon of publicity.

*

Not to encumber the earth— No pathetic Excelsior, but just this: not to encumber the earth.*

*

---

* The thought is taken from the posthumously published papers of Bertil Ekman (1894–1920), who died on a mountain-climbing expedition. His idealism and rigorist Kierkegaardian ethics exerted a powerful influence on H. as a young man. W. H. A.

To exist in the fleet joy of becoming, to be a channel for life as it flashes by in its gaiety and courage, cool water glittering in the sunlight—in a world of sloth, anxiety, and aggression.

To exist for the future of others without being suffocated by their present.

*

How far both from muscular heroism and from the soulfully tragic spirit of unselfishness which unctuously adds its little offering to the spongecake at a *Kaffeeklatsch,* is the plain simple fact that a man has given himself completely to something he finds worth living for.

*

Dare he, for whom circumstances make it possible to realize his true destiny, refuse it simply because he is not prepared to give up everything else?

*

The man who is unwilling to accept the axiom that he who chooses one path is denied the others must try to persuade himself, I suppose, that the logical thing to do is to remain at the crossroads.

But do not blame the man who does take a path— nor commend him, either.

A young man, adamant in his committed life. The one who was nearest to him relates how, on the last evening, he arose from supper, laid aside his garments, and washed the feet of his friends and disciples—an adamant young man, alone as he confronted his final destiny.

He had observed their mean little play for his—his!—friendship. He knew that not one of them had the slightest conception why he had to act in the way that he must. He knew how frightened and shaken they would all be. And one of them had informed on him, and would probably soon give a signal to the police.

He had assented to a possibility in his being, of which he had had his first inkling when he returned from the desert. If God required anything of him, he would not fail. Only recently, he thought, had he begun to see more clearly, and to realize that the road of possibility might lead to the Cross. He knew, though, that he had to follow it, still uncertain as to whether he was indeed "the one who shall bring it to pass," but certain that the answer could only be learned by following the road to the end. The end *might* be a death without significance—as well as being the end of the road of possibility.

Well, then, the last evening. An adamant young man: "Know ye what I have done to you? . . . And now I have told you before it come to pass. . . . One of you shall betray me. . . . Whither I go, ye cannot come. . . . Will'st thou lay down thy life for my sake? Verily I say unto thee: the cock shall not crow. . . . My peace I give unto you. . . . That the world may know that I love the Father, and as the Father gave me commandment, even so I do. . . . Arise, let us go hence."*

Is the hero of this immortal, brutally simple drama in truth "the Lamb of God that taketh away the sins of the world"? Absolutely faithful to a divined possibility —in that sense the Son of God, in that sense the sacrificial Lamb, in that sense the Redeemer. A young man, adamant in his commitment, who walks the road of possibility to the end without self-pity or demand for sympathy, fulfilling the destiny he has chosen—even sacrificing affection and fellowship when the others are unready to follow him—into a new fellowship.

*

Assenting to his possibility—why? Does he sacrifice himself for others, *yet for his own sake*—in megalomania? Or does he realize himself for the sake of others? The difference is that between a monster and a man. "A new commandment I give unto you: that ye love one another."

*

The inner possibility—in dangerous interplay with an external one. The road of possibility had led to the shouts of Hosanna at his entry into the city—shouts which opened up other possibilities than the one he had chosen.

*

* H. quotes from John 13 and 14 in Swedish. I have used the Authorized version. W. H. A.

That our pains and longings are thousandfold and can be anesthetized in a thousand different ways is as commonplace a truth as that, in the end, they are all *one,* and can only be overcome in *one way.* What you most need is to feel—or believe you feel—that you are needed.

Fated or chosen—in the end, the vista of future loneliness only allows a choice between two alternatives: either to despair in desolation, or to stake so high on the "possibility" that one acquires the right to life in a transcendental co-inherence. But doesn't choosing the second call for the kind of faith which moves mountains?

A sunny day in March. Within the birch tree's slender shadow on the crust of snow, the freezing stillness of the air is crystallized. Then—all of a sudden—the first blackbird's piercing note of call, a reality outside yourself, the real world. All of a sudden—the Earthly Paradise from which we have been excluded by our knowledge.

*

He came with his little girl. She wore her best frock. You noticed what good care she took of it. Others noticed too—idly noticed that, last year, it had been the best frock on another little girl.

In the morning sunshine it had been festive. Now most people had gone home. The balloon sellers were counting the day's takings. Even the sun had followed their example, and retired to rest behind a cloud. So the place looked rather bleak and deserted when he came with his little girl to taste the joy of Spring and warm himself in the freshly polished Easter sun.

But she was happy. They both were. They had learned a humility of which you still have no conception. A humility which never makes comparisons, never rejects what there is for the sake of something "else" or something "more."

Lean fare, austere forms,
Brief delight, few words.
Low down in cool space
One star—
The morning star.
In the pale light of sparseness
Lives the Real Thing,
And we are real.

*

Upon your continual cowardice, your repeated lies, sentence will be passed on the day when some exhibition of your weakness, in itself, perhaps, quite trivial, deprives you of any further opportunities to make a choice—and justly.

Do you at least feel grateful that your trial is permitted to continue, that you have not yet been taken at your word?

*

As a climber you will have a wide sphere of activity even after, if that should happen, you reach your goal. You can, for instance, try to prevent others from becoming better qualified than yourself.

*

It occurs to you in a flash: *I might just as well never have existed.* Other people, however, seeing you with a guaranteed salary, a bank account, and a briefcase under your arm, assume that you take your existence for granted. *What* you are can be of interest to them, not *that* you are. Your pension—not your death—is what you should think about "while the day lasts."

*

> *The fuss you make is far too much;*
> *I really have no need of such.*
> (BIRGER SJÖBERG)

If even dying is to be made a social function, then, please, grant me the favor of sneaking out on tiptoe without disturbing the party.

*

X—outwardly restless, inwardly ascetic, in feeling anti-feminine. Concordant aspects of a single personality, but without any causal connection between them. While "more normal" types, when they venture out under the open sky, drag along with them the atmosphere of the office and the bedroom, in his company you can escape into a world of freedom and reality even within thick walls or under a low ceiling. His touch is light, but more unerring and sensitive than that of others. An inflection of his voice can bind, a glance unite.

My friend, the Popular Psychologist, is certain of his diagnosis. And has understood nothing, nothing.

*

Spiritual liberation has its sensual component, just as claustrophobia of the soul has its physical symbolism and physiological ground.

*

The courage not to betray what is noblest in oneself is considered, at best, to be pride. And the critic finds his judgment confirmed when he sees consequences which, to him, must look very like the punishment for a mortal sin.

*

The irredeemable in a man of power: vice versa, the power of the redeemed.

*

Where does the frontier lie? Where do we travel to in those dreams of beauty satisfied, laden with significance but without comprehensible meaning, etched far deeper on the mind than any witness of the eyes? Where all is well—without fear, without desire.

Our memories of physical reality, where do they vanish to? While the images of this dream world never grow older. They live—like the memory of a memory.

For example, my bird dream. Or my dreams about the night and the morning.

*

Weary birds, large weary birds, perched upon a tremendous cliff that rises out of dark waters, await the fall of night. Weary birds turn their heads towards the blaze in the west. The glow turns to blood, the blood is mixed with soot. We look out across the waters towards the west and upward into the soaring arch of the sunset. Stillness— Our lives are one with that of this huge far-off world, as it makes its entry into the night. —Our few words, spoken or unspoken (My words? His words?), die away: now it is too dark for us to find the way back.

*

Night. The road stretches ahead. Behind me it winds up in curves towards the house, a gleam in the darkness under the dense trees of the park. I know that, shrouded in the dark out there, people are moving, that all around me, hidden by the night, life is a-quiver. I know that something is waiting for me in the house. Out of the darkness of the park comes the call of a solitary bird: and I go—up there.

*

Light without a visible source, the pale gold of a new day. Low bushes, their soft silk-gray leaves silvered with dew. All over the hills, the cool red of the cat's-foot in flower. A blue horizon. Emerging from the ravine where a brook runs under a canopy of leaves, I walk out onto a wide open slope. Drops, sprinkled by swaying branches, glitter on my hands, cool my forehead, and evaporate in the gentle morning breeze.

*

Now. When I have overcome my fears—of others, of myself, of the underlying darkness:

at the frontier of the unheard-of.

Here ends the known. But, from a source beyond it, something fills my being with its possibilities.

Here desire is purified and made lucid: each action is a preparation for, each choice an assent to the unknown.

Prevented by the duties of life on the surface from looking down into the depths, yet all the while being slowly trained and molded by them to take the plunge into the deep whence rises the fragrance of a forest star, bearing the promise of a new affection.

At the frontier—

*

When you have reached the point where you no longer expect a response, you will at last be able to give in such a way that the other is able to receive, and be grateful. When Love has matured and, through a dissolution of the self into light, become a radiance, then shall the Lover be liberated from dependence upon the Beloved, and the Beloved also be made perfect by being liberated from the Lover.

*

In what dimension of time is this feeling eternal? It was, it filled me with its treasures. Born in me, known to none, it fled from me—yet was created, beyond space and time, from a heart of flesh and blood which shall presently become dust.

*

So rests the sky against the earth. The dark still tarn in the lap of the forest. As a husband embraces his wife's body in faithful tenderness, so the bare ground and trees are embraced by the still, high, light of the morning.

I feel an ache of longing to share in this embrace, to be united and absorbed. A longing like carnal desire, but directed towards earth, water, sky, and returned by the whispers of the trees, the fragrance of the soil, the caresses of the wind, the embrace of water and light. Content? No, no, no—but refreshed, rested—while waiting.

*

He received—nothing. But for that he paid more than others for their treasures.

*

To separate himself from the society of which he was
born a member will lead the revolutionary, not to life
but to death, unless, in his very revolt, he is driven by
a love of what, seemingly, must be rejected, and therefore, at the profoundest level, remains faithful to that
society.

*

In the Devil's pack, the cards of malediction and death
lie next to the cards of success. It is only the cards of
love which are missing— Does he himself understand
that this is the reason why he decides the fate of so
many? For one, he is a God-surrogate. For another, a
tyrant who must be fought.

*

How easy Psychology has made it for us to dismiss the
perplexing mystery with a label which assigns it a place
in the list of common aberrations.

*

What happens during the unspoken dialogue between
two people can never be put right by anything they say
—not even if, with mutual insight into what has occurred, they should make a joint attempt at reparation.

*

The extrahuman in the experience of the greatness of
Nature. This does not allow itself to be reduced to an
expression of our human reactions, nor can we share
in it by expressing them. Unless we each find a way to
chime in as one note in the organic whole, we shall
only observe ourselves observing the interplay of its
thousand components in a harmony outside our experience of it as harmony.

Landscape: only your immediate experience of the
detail can provide the soil in your soul where the
beauty of the whole can grow.

*

The sacrament of the arctic summer night: an odor of
ice and bursting buds—the rust-brown gleam of bare
tree trunks, the glitter of fresh resinous leaves—the lap
of water in the open channels, the warbling of the
willow wren—the deathly gleam of ice blocks in the
slanting rays of the sun—the rhododendrons breaking
in a purple wave up the mooring beach—here and there
in the sere scrub, white dots of Pinguicula, like drops
of cool sunlit water. Victory—

*

Humility before the flower at the timber line is the gate
which gives access to the path up the open fell.

*

Excited by the thought of a further sacrifice because life
has still not demanded all. Suppose, though, it has already taken all it can use. The wish to give everything
is all very fine, provided you have succeeded in so
enriching your soul that everything you have to offer is
of value. If not— And why so tense? What currents of
worldly ambition still course through your striving as
a human being?

*

Autumn in the wilderness: life as an end in itself, even in the annihilation of the individual life, the distant vistas clear, the neighborhood calm, at the moment of its extinction—this evening I would say Yes to the execution squad, not out of exhaustion or defiance, but with an untroubled faith in the co-inherence of all things—to sustain this faith in my life among men.

*

Autumn in Lapland. The warm rain-laden east wind rushes down the dried-up river bed. On its banks, yellowing birches tremble in the storm.

The opening bars in the great hymn of extinction. Not a hymn to extinction or because of it. Not a hymn in spite of extinction. But a dying which is the hymn.

*

"At the frontier of the unheard-of—" The unheard-of—perhaps this simply refers to Lord Jim's last meeting with Doramin, when he has attained absolute courage and humility in an absolute loyalty towards himself. Conscious of guilt, but at the same time conscious of having atoned, so far as atonement is possible in this life—by what he has done for those who are now asking for his life. Untroubled and happy. Like someone wandering by himself along a lonely seashore.

1952

—¤——¤——¤——¤—

"Night is drawing nigh—" How long the road is. But, for all the time the journey has already taken, how you have needed every second of it in order to learn what the road passes—by.

❋

"I am being led further"—Yes, yes—but you have not been blind to the main chance.

❋

"Thy will be done—" Admittedly, you have allowed self-interest to supply the energy for your little efforts to assist fate; admittedly, to others you have tried to paint these efforts in the most glowing colors—no matter, provided only that you allow the final outcome to be decided entirely over your head, in faith.

"Thy will be done—" To let the inner take precedence over the outer, the soul over the world—wherever this may lead you. And, lest a worldly good should disguise itself as a spiritual, to make yourself blind to the value the life of the spirit can bestow upon life in this world.

❋

Work as an anesthetic against loneliness, books as a substitute for people—! You say you are waiting, that the door stands open. For what? People? Is not the Etna for which Empedocles is waiting, a fate beyond human companionship?

*

The hardest thing of all—to die *rightly*. —An exam nobody is spared—and how many pass it? And you? You pray for strength to meet the test—but also for leniency on the part of the Examiner.

*

Birth and death, love and pain—the reality behind the dance under the daylight lamps of social responsibility.

How well I understand the mirror symbolism in Cocteau's *Orphée*. To break through the barrier which, when I encounter reality, prevents my encountering myself—to break through it, even at the price of having to enter the Kingdom of Death. Nevertheless—what do I long for more ardently than just this? When and how shall I find the occasion to do it? Or is it already too late?

Is my contact with others anything more than a contact with reflections? Who or what can give me the power to transform the mirror into a doorway?

Chance? Necessity? Am I not too "sensible and well-balanced," that is to say, too self-centered socially to surrender to anything less than a necessity? One which can be accounted for!

"At the frontier of the unheard-of—" Aware of the *consummatio* of the deep-sea dive—but afraid, by instinct, experience, education, for "certain reasons," of putting my head under water, ignorant, even, of how it is done.

*

The stream of life through millions of years, the stream of human lives through countless centuries. Evil, death and dearth, sacrifice and love—what does "I" mean in such a perspective? Reason tells me that I am bound to seek my own good, seek to gratify my desires, win power for myself and admiration from others. And yet I "know"—know without knowing—that, in such a perspective, nothing could be less important. A vision in which God *is*.

*

To preserve the silence within—amid all the noise. To remain open and quiet, a moist humus in the fertile darkness where the rain falls and the grain ripens—no matter how many tramp across the parade ground in whirling dust under an arid sky.

*

When the sense of the earth unites with the sense of one's body, one becomes earth of the earth, a plant among plants, an animal born from the soil and fertilizing it. In this union, the body is confirmed in its pantheism.

*

It is easy to be nice, even to an enemy—from lack of character.

*

Is your disgust at your emptiness to be the only life with which you fill it?

*

Now you have been there—and it wasn't much. Throughout life, how many steps must we take, how many hours must we spend, in order to have heard, to have seen—what?

*

Is in the void,
Sleeps in the silence,
Cries in the dark—
Little incubus,
When, *when?*

*

Now you know. When the worries over your work loosen their grip, then this experience of light, warmth, and power. From without—a sustaining element, like air to the glider or water to the swimmer. An intellectual hesitation which demands proofs and logical demonstration prevents me from "believing"—in this, too. Prevents me from expressing and interpreting this reality in intellectual terms. Yet, through me there flashes this vision of a magnetic field in the soul, created in a timeless present by unknown multitudes, living in holy obedience, whose words and actions are a timeless prayer.

—"The Communion of Saints"—and—within it—an eternal life.

*

Never, "for the sake of peace and quiet," deny your own experience or convictions.

*

Give me something to die for—!

The walls stand
Speechless and cold, the banners
Faffle in the wind.   *(Hölderlin)*

What makes loneliness an anguish
Is not that I have no one to share my burden,
But this:
I have only my own burden to bear.

*

Incapable of being blinded by desire,
Feeling I have no right to intrude upon another,
Afraid of exposing my own nakedness,
Demanding complete accord as a condition for a life to-
        gether:
How could things have gone otherwise?

*

Pray that your loneliness may spur you into finding
something to live for, great enough to die for.

*

Fatigue dulls the pain, but awakes enticing thoughts of
death. So! *that* is the way in which you are tempted to
overcome your loneliness—by making the ultimate escape from life. —No! It may be that death is to be
your ultimate gift to life: it must not be an act of
treachery against it.

"Give yourself"—in your work, for others: by all
means so long as you don't do this self-consciously
(with, perhaps, even an expectation of being admired
for it).

*

What I ask for is absurd: that life shall have a meaning.
   What I strive for is impossible: that my life shall acquire a meaning.
   I dare not believe, I do not see how I shall ever be
able to believe: that I am not alone.

*

Is the bleakness of this world of mine a reflection of
my poverty or my honesty, a symptom of weakness or
of strength, an indication that I have strayed from my
path, or that I am following it? —Will despair provide
the answer?

*

72

"—a meaning." When a seventeen-year-old speaks of this, he is ridiculous, because he has no idea what he is talking about. Now, at the age of forty-seven, I am ridiculous because my knowledge of exactly what I am putting down on paper does not stop me from doing so.

*

How ridiculous, this need of yours to communicate! Why should it mean so much to you that at least *one* person has seen the inside of your life? Why should you write down all this, for yourself, to be sure—*perhaps,* though, for others as well?

*

Loneliness is not the sickness unto death. No, but can it be cured except by death? And does it not become the harder to bear the closer one comes to death?

1953

————

"—Night is drawing nigh—"
For all that has been—Thanks!
To all that shall be—Yes!

*

Maturity: among other things—not to hide one's strength out of fear and, consequently, live below one's best.

*

Goodness is something so simple: always to live for others, never to seek one's own advantage.

*

When in decisive moments—as now—God acts, it is with a stern purposefulness, a Sophoclean irony. When the hour strikes, He takes what is His. What have *you* to say? —Your prayer has been answered, as you know. God has a use for you, even though what He asks doesn't happen to suit you at the moment. God, who "abases him whom He raises up."

*

74

> Will it come, or will it not,
> The day when the joy becomes great,
> The day when the grief becomes small?
> *(Gunnar Ekelöf)*

*

It *did* come—the day when the grief became small. For what had befallen me and seemed so hard to bear became insignificant in the light of the demands which God was now making. But how difficult it is to feel that this was also, and for that very reason, the day when the joy became great.

*

Not I, but God in me.

*

Maturity: among other things, a new lack of self-consciousness—the kind you can only attain when you have become entirely indifferent to yourself through an absolute assent to your fate.

He who has placed himself in God's hand stands free vis-à-vis men: he is entirely at his ease with them, because he has granted them the right to judge.

*

April 7, 1953

"Their lives grounded in and sustained by God, they are incapable of any kind of pride; because they give back to God all the benefits He has bestowed on them, they do not glorify each other, but do all things to the Glory of God alone." *(Thomas à Kempis)*

*

I am the vessel. The draught is God's. And God is the thirsty one.

*

In the last analysis, what does the word "sacrifice" mean? Or even the word "gift"? He who has nothing can give nothing. The gift is God's—to God.

*

He who has surrendered himself to it knows that the Way ends on the Cross—even when it is leading him through the jubilation of Gennesaret or the triumphal entry into Jerusalem.

*

To be free, to be able to stand up and leave *everything* behind—without looking back. To say *Yes*—

*

Except in faith, nobody is humble. The mask of weakness or of Phariseeism is not the naked face of humility.

And, except in faith, nobody is proud. The vanity displayed in all its varieties by the spiritually immature is not pride.

To be, in faith, both humble and proud: that is, to *live,* to know that in God I am nothing, but that God is in me.

*

To say Yes to life is at one and the same time to say Yes to oneself.

Yes—even to that element in one which is most unwilling to let itself be transformed from a temptation into a strength.

*

76

That strange moment when a man's features are dissolved into the trembling shimmer on the surface of the wave, through which you peer into the depths without being able to see the bottom. You are tempted to dive in and to grasp—but the water cannot be grasped, and beneath its surface you cannot breathe. One step further and the relation is destroyed, reduced to terror and error: you imagine you are taking possession of a human being, but, in fact, you are losing him. In your attempt to break down the boundaries of a personality, you are building a new prison for yourself.

*

Below even the sunniest and most secure human relationship, the abyss lies waiting—because our lack of faith is fascinated by the possibilities of the night side of life.

*

A landscape can sing about God, a body about Spirit.

*

Maturity: among other things, the unclouded happiness of the child at play, who takes it for granted that he is at one with his playmates.

*

A human intimacy—free from the earth, but blessing the earth.

*

If only I may grow: firmer, simpler—quieter, warmer.

*

Your life is without a foundation if, in any matter, you choose on your own behalf.

*

The humility which comes from others having faith in you.

1954

―――――――――

"—Night is drawing nigh—"
Let me finish what I have been permitted to begin.
Let me give all without any assurance of increase.

*

The pride of the cup is in the drink, its humility in the serving. What, then, do its defects matter?

*

Salty and wind-swept, but warm and glittering. Keeping in step with the measure under the fixed stars of the task. How many personal failures are due to a lack of faith in this harmony between human beings, at once strict and gentle.

*

With all the powers of your body concentrated in the
    hand on the tiller,
All the powers of your mind concentrated on the goal
    beyond the horizon,
You laugh as the salt spray catches your face in the
    second of rest
Before a new wave—
Sharing the happy freedom of the moment with those
    who share your responsibility.
So—in the self-forgetfulness of concentrated atten-
    tion—the door opens for you into a pure living
    intimacy,
A shared, timeless happiness,
Conveyed by a smile,
A wave of the hand.

    Thanks to those who have taught me this. Thanks to
the days which have taught me this.

*

Then I saw that the wall had never been there, that the
"unheard-of" is here and this, not something and somewhere else,
    that the "offering" is here and now, always and
everywhere—"surrendered" *to be* what, in me, God
gives of Himself to Himself.

*

Only he who at every moment is all he is capable of
being can hope for a furlough from the frontier before
he disappears into the darkness. The sentinels of the
Enemy do not sleep.

*

"Faith is the marriage of God and the Soul." *(St. John of the Cross)*

Faith *is:* it cannot, therefore, be comprehended, far less identified with, the formulae in which we paraphrase what is.

—*"en una noche oscura."* The Dark Night of the Soul—so dark that we may not even look for faith. The night in Gethsemane when the last friends left you have fallen asleep, all the others are seeking your downfall, and *God is silent,* as the marriage is consummated.

＊

To be governed by that which comes alive when we have ceased to live—as interested parties or as know-it-alls. To be able to see, hear, and attend to that within us which *is* there in the darkness and the silence.

＊

Tomorrow, you will have to play a much more difficult piece—tomorrow, when the audience is beginning to listen for wrong notes, and you no longer have me in the wings. Then we shall see what you can really do.

＊

The responsibility for our mistakes is ours, but not the credit for our achievements. Man's freedom is a freedom to betray God. God may love us—yes—but our response is voluntary.

＊

Your responsibility is a "to—": you can never save yourself by a "not-to—."

＊

81

A crack in the jug? Then you have let it get cold.

*

Thou* who has created us free, Who seest all that happens—yet art confident of victory,
    Thou who at this time art the one among us who
    suffereth the uttermost loneliness,
    Thou—who art also in me,
    May I bear Thy burden, when my hour comes,
    May I—

*

Regard yourself as an exception, if you like: but, in
that case, abandon your hope of finding "rest in that
Peace which has created the world." *(Karin Boye)*

*

The body: not a thing, not "his" or "hers," not an
instrument of action or desire. In its utter nakedness—
Man.

*

Beside our need for a meaning, also a need for human
intimacy without conventional trappings—for the experience of a circle where power expresses itself in
meaningful and beautiful forms. The holiness of human life, before which we bow down in worship.

*

Blood, grime, sweat, earth—where are these in the
world you desire? Everywhere—the ground from which
the flame ascends straight upwards.

*

---

* Swedish, like German, has the intimate second person singular.
Consequently, H. uses *Du* both when addressing God and when addressing himself. I have followed the English convention of only
using the *Thou* forms when God is addressed. W. H. A.

Offspring of the past, pregnant with the future, the present moment, nevertheless, always exists in eternity —always in eternity as the point of intersection between time and the timelessness of faith, and, therefore, as the moment of freedom from past and future.

Thou who art over us,
Thou who art one of us,
Thou who *art*—
Also within us,
May all see Thee—in me also,
May I prepare the way for Thee,
May I thank Thee for all that shall fall to my lot,
May I also not forget the needs of others,
Keep me in Thy love
As Thou wouldest that all should be kept in mine.
May everything in this my being he directed to Thy
       glory
And may I never despair
For I am under Thy hand,
And in Thee is all power and goodness.

Give me a pure heart—that I may see Thee,
A humble heart—that I may hear Thee,
A heart of love—that I may serve Thee,
A heart of faith—that I may abide in Thee.

*

The "unheard-of"—to be in the hands of God.
   Once again a reminder that this is all that remains for you to live for—and once more the feeling of disappointment which shows how slow you are to learn.

*

Never at your destination. —The greater task is only a higher class in this school, as you draw closer to your final exam, which nobody else will know about, because then you will be *completely alone.*

*

Yes, God tempts—with "equality," with every virtue that allows itself to be used for other purposes than His glory. The more He demands of us, the more dangerous are the raw materials He has given us for our achievement. Thank Him then—His gift is also the keys to the Gates of Hell.

> Righteous in Thine eyes,
> With Thy courage,
> Within Thy peace.

*

"For man shall commune with all creatures to his profit, but enjoy God alone." That is why no human being can be a permanent source of happiness to another.

*

So long as you abide in the Unheard-of, you are beyond and above—to hold fast to this must be the First Commandment in your spiritual discipline.

*

12.10

"*God spake once,* and twice I have also heard the same: that power belongeth unto God;

and that thou, Lord, art merciful: for thou rewardest every man according to his work."* *(Psalm 62:11, 12)*

*

12.25

To have faith—not to hesitate!

*

12.30

"If I take the wings of the morning and remain in the uttermost parts of the sea;

even there also shall thy hand lead me." *(Psalm 139:8)*

---

* When H. quotes from the Psalms, he always quotes in English and always uses the version in the Anglican Psaltery. He had in his library, now in the Royal Library, Stockholm, an edition of *The Book of Common Prayer* dated 1762, the working of which is now and again slightly different from the book in current use. This may account for some of H.'s occasional departures from the current text, but not for all. These are so slight and insignificant—some, I am sure, just slips of the memory—that I have taken the liberty of correcting them. W. H. A.

1955

—▪—▪—▪—

"Nought is given 'neath the sun,
Nought is had that is not won."
(Swedish hymn)

✻

Rumi: The lovers of God have no religion but God alone.

✻

"The purer the eye of her attention, the more power the soul finds within herself. But it is very rare to find a soul who is entirely free, whose purity is not soiled by the stain of some secret desire of her own. Strive, then, constantly to purify the eye of your attention until it becomes utterly simple and direct."

✻

On a really clean tablecloth, the smallest speck of dirt annoys the eye. At high altitudes, a moment's self-indulgence may mean death.

✻

"To the pure all things are pure." But if a man can only reach this state by making compromises, then his striving is itself an impurity. In such matters there are no differences of degree.

"What! *He* is now going to try to teach *me!*" —Why not? There is nobody from whom you cannot learn. Before God, who speaks through all men, you are always in the bottom class of nursery school.

*

Before Thee in humility, with Thee in faith, in Thee in peace.

*

So, once again, you chose for yourself—and opened the door to chaos. The chaos you become whenever God's hand does not rest upon your head.

He who has once been under God's hand, has lost his innocence: only he feels the full explosive force of destruction which is released by a moment's surrender to temptation.

But when his attention is directed beyond and above, how strong he is, with the strength of God who is within him because he is in God. Strong and free, because his self no longer exists.

*

How would the moral sense of Reason—and of Society —have evolved without the martyrs to the faith? Indeed, how could this moral sense have escaped withering away, had it not constantly been watered by the feeder-stream of power that issues from those who have forgotten themselves in God? The rope over the abyss is held taut by those who, faithful to a faith which is the perpetual ultimate sacrifice, give it anchorage in Heaven.

Those whose souls are married to God have been declared the salt of the earth—woe betide them, if the salt should lose its savor.

*

To say Yes is never more difficult than when circumstances prevent you from rushing to the defense of someone whose purity of heart makes him defenseless before an attack.

*

During a working day, which is real only in God, the only poetry which can be real to you is the kind which makes you become real under God: only then is the poetry real for *you,* the art true. You no longer have time for—pastimes.

*

Your position never gives you the right to command. It only imposes on you the duty of so living your life that others can receive your orders without being humiliated.

*

Your errors of the past make your relation to others difficult when the present shows you that you might repeat them.

*

The only kind of dignity which is genuine is that which is not diminished by the indifference of others.

❋

There is a pride of faith, more unforgivable and dangerous than the pride of the intellect. It reveals a split personality in which faith is "observed" and appraised, thus negating that unity born of a dying-unto-self, which is the definition of faith. To "value" faith is to turn it into a metaphysical magic, the advantages of which ought to be reserved for a spiritual elite.

❋

Prayer, crystallized in words, assigns a permanent wave length on which the dialogue has to be continued, even when our mind is occupied with other matters.

❋

Furnishing this house as your second home is like furnishing a grave-chamber: you know that you will never *live* here—not after what you have learned.

In the old days, Death was always one of the party. Now he sits next to me at the dinner table: I have to make friends with him.

❋

In this intuitive "anamnesis" which has become my Ariadne's thread through life—step by step, day by day—the end is now as real to me as tomorrow morning's foreseen task.

❋

"To listen"—in faith—to find one's way and have the feeling that, under God, one is really finding it again.

This is like playing blindman's buff: deprived of sight, I have, in compensation, to sharpen all my other senses, to grope my way and recognize myself as I pass my fingers over the faces of my friends, and thus find what was mine already and had been there all the time. What I would have known all the time was there, had I not blindfolded myself.

*

In a dream: encountering an earlier experience with the same causal relations to past and future which our experiences in waking life have—but which, nevertheless, were only relations in a dream.

*

7.29.55

Thomas à Kempis: Why do you seek rest? You were only created to labor.

*

Shame mixed with gratitude: shame over all my bouts of vanity, envy, and self-complacency—gratitude for all to which my bare intention, though certainly not my achievement, may possibly have entitled me.

God sometimes allows us to take the credit—for His work. Or withdraws from it into His solitude. He watches our capers on the stage with an ironic smile—so long as we do not tamper with the scales of justice.

*

"Thine. . ." A sacrifice—and a liberation—to obey a will for which "I" is in no respect a goal!

"Destined. . ." A reward—or a price—to be committed to a task in comparison with which nothing I could seek for myself is of any value.

*

You listen badly, and you read even worse. Except when the talk or the book is about yourself. Then you pay careful attention. Are you so observant *of* yourself?

*

8.1.55

"God spake. . . . ."
And, a few verses earlier: "As for the children of men, they are but vanity. The children of men are deceitful upon the weights. Give not yourselves unto vanity." *(Psalm 62:9, 10)*

*

"Not unto us, O Lord, but unto thy name give the praise . . ." *(Psalm 115:1)*
A troubled spirit? Isn't the cause obvious? As soon as, furtively, you sought honor for yourself, you could no longer transform your weakness into strength. So you were "led into temptation," and lost that certainty of faith which makes saying Yes to fate a self-evident necessity, for such certainty presupposes that it is not grounded in any sort of a lie.

*

91

Do you still need to evoke memories of a self-imposed humiliation in order to extinguish a smoldering self-admiration?

To be pure in heart means, among other things, to have freed yourself from all such half-measures: from a tone of voice which places you in the limelight, a furtive acceptance of some desire of the flesh which ignores the desire of the spirit, a self-righteous reaction to others in their moments of weakness.

Look at yourself in *that* mirror when you wish to be praised—or to judge. Do so without despairing.

*

It is not sufficient to place yourself daily under God. What really matters is to be *only* under God: the slightest division of allegiance opens the door to daydreaming, petty conversation, petty boasting, petty malice—all the petty satellites of the death-instinct.

"But how, then, am I to love God?" "You must love Him as if He were a non-God, a non-Spirit, a non-Person, a non-Substance: love Him simply as the One, the pure and absolute Unity in which is no trace of Duality. And into this One, we must let ourselves fall continually from being into non-being. God helps us to do this."

*

You are dedicated to this task—because of the Divine intention behind what is, in fact, only a sacrificial rite in a still barbarian cult: a feeble creation of men's hands—but you have to give your all to this human dream for the sake of that which alone gives it reality.

*

He broke fresh ground—because, and only because, he had the courage to go ahead without asking whether others were following or even understood. He had no need for the divided responsibility in which others seek to be safe from ridicule, because he had been granted a faith which required no confirmation—a contact with reality, light and intense like the touch of a loved hand: a union in self-surrender without self-destruction, where his heart was lucid and his mind loving. In sun and wind, how near and how remote— How different from what the knowing ones call Mysticism.

*

A task becomes a duty from the moment you suspect it to be an essential part of that integrity which alone entitles a man to assume responsibility.

*

The style of conduct which carries weight calls for stubbornness even in an act of concession: you have to be severe with yourself in order to have the right to be gentle to others.

*

"Those scarred by suffering, those who have beheld—" You can, if you choose, enter into their consciousness and learn—without having gone through their hard school—to see and hear like one who "hath not" and from whom "shall be taken away even that which he hath."

*

The scientist only records what he has been able to establish as indisputable fact. In the same way, only what is unique in a person's experience is worth writing down as a guide and a warning to others. In the same way, too, an explorer leaves it to others to pass their time taking notes on the quaint customs of the natives, or making devastating remarks about the foibles of their traveling companions.

True—and which do you do?

*

While performing the part which is truly ours, how exhausting it is to be obliged to play a role which is not ours: the person you must really be in order to fulfill your task, you must not appear to others to be, in order to be allowed by them to fulfill it. How exhausting—but unavoidable, since mankind has laid down once and for all the organized rules for social behavior.

*

Respect for the word is the first commandment in the discipline by which a man can be educated to maturity —intellectual, emotional, and moral.

Respect for the word—to employ it with scrupulous care and an incorruptible heartfelt love of truth—is essential if there is to be any growth in a society or in the human race.

To misuse the word is to show contempt for man. It undermines the bridges and poisons the wells. It causes Man to regress down the long path of his evolution.

"But I say unto you, that every idle word that men speak. . . ."

11.19–20.55

The light died in the low clouds. Falling snow drank in the dusk. Shrouded in silence, the branches wrapped me in their peace. When the boundaries were erased, once again the wonder: that *I* exist.

*

"Concerning men and their way to peace and concord—?" The truth is so simple that it is considered a pretentious banality. Yet it is continually being denied by our behavior. Every day furnishes new examples.

It is more important to be aware of the grounds for your own behavior than to understand the motives of another.

The other's "face" is more important than your own. If, while pleading another's cause, you are at the same time seeking something for yourself, you cannot hope to succeed.

You can only hope to find a lasting solution to a conflict if you have learned to see the other objectively, but, at the same time, to experience his difficulties subjectively.

The man who "likes people" disposes once and for all of the man who despises them.

All first-hand experience is valuable, and he who has given up looking for it will one day find—that he lacks what he needs: a closed mind is a weakness, and he who approaches persons or painting or poetry without the youthful ambition to learn a new language and so gain access to someone else's perspective on life, let him beware.

A successful lie is doubly a lie, an error which has to be corrected is a heavier burden than truth: only an uncompromising "honesty" can reach the bedrock of decency which you should always expect to find, even under deep layers of evil.

Diplomatic "finesse" must never be another word for fear of being unpopular: that is to seek the appearance of influence at the cost of its reality.

*

Always fleeing,
always *waiting*.
Prepared—when shall I confront my—
Images, images—secretly related.
Creating or destroying, in life, in dream,
In art.

*

Le courage de nos différences. Without becoming irresponsible, to accept what divides us—with humility and pride. It is by the "new" that mankind is saved or betrayed.

*

Even in the most intense activity, this feeling of unreality—in you who have never come "close" to another. The old fairy tale: the one who has been made invisible or transformed into a beast can only regain his human shape through somebody else's love.

*

A jealous dream which refuses to share you with anybody or anything else: the greatest creation of mankind—the dream of mankind.

The greatest creation of mankind, in which it is the noblest dream of the individual—to lose himself.

Therefore: gladly death or humiliation if that is what the dream demands.

Therefore: how easy to forgive.

*

"Thou art the God that doest wonders: and hast declared thy power among the peoples." *(Psalm 77:14)*

*

Coquettish—even in taking note of your coquettishness.

*

Alone beside the moorland spring, once again you are aware of your loneliness—as it is and always has been. As it always has been—even when, at times, the friendship of others veiled its nakedness.

But the spring is alive. And your sentry duty remains to you.

*

Really, nothing was easier than to step from one rope ladder to the other—over the chasm. But, in your dream, you failed, because the thought occurred to you that you might possibly fall.

*

Aladdin— However great the price you paid, luckbringer, it was not too much for that which to you is the source of all joy, and to the crowd appears to be your "good luck."

*

The everlastingness of things—an ironic commentary upon your claims to ownership.

12.24.55

"O God, thou art my God . . .
. . . in a barren and dry land where no water is. Thus
have I looked for thee in the sanctuary, that I might
behold thy power and glory." *(Psalm 63:1–3)*

*

Two old inklings, the far-reaching significance of which
I have only recently perceived.
    Through the senses,
    But beyond them.
    Near,
    Even though far off.
    The look a shy caress,
    As their eyes met in complete understanding.
And:
The Lover desires the perfection of the Beloved—which
requires, among other things, the liberation of the Be-
loved from the Lover.

*

God desires our independence—which we attain when,
ceasing to strive for it ourselves, we "fall" back into
God.

*

12.25.55

"But when in this way they taste God, be it in Himself
or in His works, they recognize at the same time that
there is an infinite distance between the creature and
the Creator, time and eternity . . . Enlighten my soul
that she may find her life and joy in Thee, until, trans-
ported out of herself by the excess of her happiness,
she binds herself to Thee with all her powers and in all
her motions."

*

Thou takest the pen—and the lines dance. Thou takest the flute—and the notes shimmer. Thou takest the brush—and the colors sing. So all things have meaning and beauty in that space beyond time where Thou art. How, then, can I hold back anything from Thee.

*

In a dream I walked with God through the deep places of creation; past walls that receded and gates that opened, through hall after hall of silence, darkness and refreshment—the dwelling place of souls acquainted with light and warmth—until, around me, was an infinity into which we all flowed together and lived anew, like the rings made by raindrops falling upon wide expanses of calm dark waters.

*

The gift burnt your hand, because it must have been far beyond the giver's means. Such indifference to "economic" considerations scorched you like a flame, because it showed up and made it impossible for you to deny your self-satisfied worldly-wise prudence: even in offering the smallest gift, you must have the *will* to give all.

*

When you are irritated by his "pretentiousness," you betray the character of your own: it is *just as it should be* that he increases while you decrease. Choose your opponents. To the wrong ones, you cannot afford to give a thought, but you must help the right ones, help them and yourself in a contest without tension.

To remain a recipient—out of humility. And preserve your flexibility.

To remain a recipient—and be grateful. Grateful for being *allowed* to listen, to observe, to understand.

*

There is a profound causal relation between the height of a man's ambition and the depth of his possible fall.

*

For him who has responded to the call of the Way of Possibility, loneliness may be obligatory. Such loneliness, it is true, may lead to a communion closer and deeper than any achieved by the union of two bodies, but your body is not going to let itself be fobbed off by a bluff: whatever you deny it, in order to follow this call, it will claim back if you fail, and claim back in forms which it will no longer be in your power to select.

It is not we who seek the Way, but the Way which seeks us. That is why you are faithful to it, even while you stand waiting, so long as you are *prepared,* and act the moment you are confronted by its demands.

*

In many matters, profound seriousness can only be expressed in words which are lighthearted, amusing, and detached; such a conversation as you may expect to hear from someone who, while deeply concerned for all things human, has nothing he is trying to gain or defend.

*

Acts of violence— Whether on a large or a small scale, the bitter paradox: the meaningfulness of death—and the meaninglessness of killing.

*

Sun and stillness. Looking down through the jade-green water, you see the monsters of the deep playing on the reef. Is this a reason to be afraid? Do you feel safer when scudding waves hide what lies beneath the surface?

*

You see deeper into him than he can himself. And you describe what you see in terms which he would reject, could he see to the bottom of his character, and reject them precisely because he could.

*

The "mystical experience." Always *here* and *now*—in that freedom which is one with distance, in that stillness which is born of silence. But—this is a freedom in the midst of action, a stillness in the midst of other human beings. The mystery is a constant reality to him who, in this world, is free from self-concern, a reality that grows peaceful and mature before the receptive attention of assent.

In our era, the road to holiness necessarily passes through the world of action.

❋

Il faut donner tout pour tout.

1956

—■—■—■—

Before Thee, Father,
    In righteousness and humility,

With Thee, Brother,
    In faith and courage,

In Thee, Spirit,
    In stillness.

Thine—for Thy will is my destiny,
  Dedicated—for my destiny is to be used and used up
according to Thy will.

✳

During these days, I have been searching my memory.
And, suddenly, I found—the smile of Mona Lisa.

It was then, an hour after her death, that I saw it—a
secret vision, a silent certainty, a peaceful joy—saw,
and thought I understood its message.

✳

Thanks to your "success," you now have something to lose. Because of this—as if suddenly aware of the risks —you ask whether you, or anyone, can "succeed." If you go on in this way, thoughtlessly mirroring yourself in an obituary, you will soon be writing your epitaph— in two senses.

*

Do what you can—and the task will rest lightly in your hand, so lightly that you will be able to look forward to the more difficult tests which may be awaiting you.

*

When the morning's freshness has been replaced by the weariness of midday, when the leg muscles quiver under the strain, the climb seems endless, and, suddenly, nothing will go quite as you wish—it is then that you must *not* hesitâte.

*

Forgiveness is the answer to the child's dream of a miracle by which what is broken is made whole again, what is soiled is again made clean. The dream explains why we need to be forgiven, and why we must forgive. In the presence of God, nothing stands between Him and us—we *are* forgiven. But we *cannot* feel His presence if anything is allowed to stand between ourselves and others.

*

—Lead us not into temptation,
But deliver us from evil:
Let all that is in me serve Thee,
And *thus* free me from all fear.

You dare your Yes—and experience a meaning.
You repeat your Yes—and all things acquire a meaning.
When everything has a meaning, how can you live anything but a *Yes.*

*

3.21.56

"Then up stood Phinehas and prayed:* and so the plague ceased. And it was counted unto him for righteousness." *(Psalm 106: 30–31)*

*

There are actions—justified only by faith—which can lift us into another sphere, where the battle is with "Principalities, Dominions and Powers." Actions upon which—out of mercy—*everything* is staked.

"For Thy holy life is our way, and your adorable patience the road by which we must approach Thee."

*

---

* *"Then up stood Phinehas and interposed. . . ."* For *interposed* H. has (like the 1762 Psalter) *prayed.* From the context it is clear that H. is thinking of Phinehas's situation as analogous to his own. I am afraid he must have been ignorant of what Phinehas actually did, which was to spear a man and a woman to death. The horrid story may be found in Numbers 25. W. H. A.

3.29.56

". . . and they loved not their lives unto the death."
(Revelations 12:11)
    Furthermore:
    "For there is mercy with thee: therefore shalt thou
be feared." *(Psalm 130:4)*
    In spite of this—and *because* of it—Gethsemane.

*

3.30.56

The third hour. And the ninth. —They are *here*. And
now. They *are* now!
    "Jesus will be in agony even to the end of the world.
We must not sleep during that time." *(Pascal)*
    We must not— And for the watcher is the far-off
present—also present in his contact with mankind
among whom, at every moment, Jesus dies in someone
who has followed the trail marks of the inner road to
the end:

> love and patience,
> > righteousness and humility,
> faith and courage,
> stillness.

*

4.8.56

"There is a contingent and non-essential will: and there
is, providential and creative, an habitual will. God has
never given Himself, and never will, to a will alien to
His own: where He finds His will, He gives Himself."
(Meister Eckhart)

*

4.22.56

Understand—through the stillness,
Act—out of the stillness,
Conquer—in the stillness.
"In order for the eye to perceive color, it must divest
itself of all colors."

*

To love life and men as God loves them—for the sake
of their infinite possibilities,
to wait like Him,
to judge like Him
without passing judgment,
to obey the order when it is given
and never look back—
then He can use you—then, *perhaps,* He will use you.
And if he doesn't use you—what matter. In His hand,
every moment has its meaning, its greatness, its glory,
its peace, its co-inherence.
From this perspective, to "believe in God" is to believe in yourself, as self-evident, as "illogical," and as
impossible to explain: if I can be, then God *is.*

*

"The blessed spirits must be sought within the self which
is common to all."

*

A poem is like a deed in that it is to be judged as a manifestation of the personality of its maker. This in no way ignores its beauty as measured by aesthetic standards of perfection, but also considers its authenticity as measured by its congruence with an inner life.

*

"The *Wind* bloweth where it listeth—
    so is everyone that is born of the spirit." *(John 3:8)*
"And the *light* shineth in darkness,
    and the darkness comprehended it not." *(John 1:5)*
   Like wind— In it, with it, *of* it. Of it just like a sail, so light and strong that, even when it is bent flat, it gathers all the power of the wind without hampering its course.
   Like light— In light, lit through by light, transformed into light. Like the lens which disappears in the light it focuses.
      Like wind. Like light.
      Just this—on these expanses, on these heights.

*

On the field where Ormuzd has challenged Ahriman to battle, he who chases away the dogs is wasting his time.

*

To rejoice at a success is not the same as taking credit for it. To deny oneself the first is to become a hypocrite and a denier of life; to permit oneself the second is a childish indulgence which will prevent one from ever growing up.

*

Beyond obedience, its attention fixed on the goal—freedom from fear.

Beyond fear—openness to life.

And beyond that—love.

*

What next? Why ask? Next will come a demand about which you already know all you need to know: that its sole measure is your own strength.

In self-defense—against the system-builders:

Your "personal" life cannot have a lasting intrinsic meaning. It can acquire a contingent meaning, but only by being fitted into and subordinated to something which "lasts" and has a meaning in itself. Is this something what we attempt to identify when we speak of "Life"? Can your life have a meaning as a tiny fragment of life?

Does Life exist? Seek and you shall find, experience Life as reality. Has Life a "meaning"? Experience Life as reality and the question becomes meaningless.

Seek—? Seek by daring to take the leap into unconditional obedience. Dare this when you are challenged, for only by the light of a challenge will you be able to see the crossroads and, in full awareness of your choice, turn your back upon your personal life—with no right ever to look back.

You will find that "in the pattern" you are liberated from the need to live "with the herd."

You will find that, thus subordinated, your life will receive from Life all its meaning, irrespective of the conditions given you for its realization.

You will find that the freedom of the continual farewell, the hourly self-surrender, gives to your experience of reality the purity and clarity which signify—self-realization.

You will find that obedience requires an act of will which must continually be reiterated, and that you will fail, if anything in your personal life is allowed to slip back into the center.

*

The "great" commitment is so much easier than the ordinary everyday one—and can all too easily shut our hearts to the latter. A willingness to make the ultimate sacrifice can be associated with, and even produce, a great hardness of heart.

You thought you were indifferent to praise for achievements which you would not yourself have counted to your credit, or that, if you should be tempted to feel flattered, you would always remember that the praise far exceeded what the events justified. You thought yourself indifferent—until you felt your jealousy flare up at his naïve attempts to "make himself important," and your self-conceit stood exposed.

Concerning the hardness of the heart—and its little-ness— Let me read with open eyes the book my days are writing—and learn.

*

6.4.56

"For He spake, and it was done: He commanded, and it stood fast." *(Psalm 33:9)*

*

6.10.56

How poor is the courage which knows its "why," compared to the quiet heroism an unreflective mind can display in the most inglorious and degrading trials.

How favored by the gods is he, whose character is tested in situations where courage has a meaning for him—perhaps, even, a tangible reward. How little does he know about his potential weakness, how easily may he be trapped and blinded by self-admiration.

*

"To have faith—not to hesitate." Also: not to doubt. "Faith is the marriage of God and the Soul." In that case, certainty of God's omnipotence *through* the soul: with God all things are possible, *because* faith can move mountains.

*

The "great" commitment all too easily obscures the "little" one. But without the humility and warmth which you have to develop in your relations to the few with whom you are personally involved, you will never be able to do anything for the many. Without them, you will live in a world of abstractions, where your solipsism, your greed for power, and your death-wish lack the one opponent which is stronger than they—love. Love, which is without an object, the outflowing of a power released by self-surrender, but which would remain a sublime sort of superhuman self-assertion, powerless against the negative forces within you, if it were not tamed by the yoke of human intimacy and warmed by its tenderness. It is better for the health of the soul to make one man good than "to sacrifice oneself for mankind." For a mature man, these are not alternatives, but two aspects of self-realization, which mutually support each, both being the outcome of one and the same choice.

*

"It *is* expedient for us, that one man should die for the people, and that the whole nation perish not." *(John 11:50)*

"Who has this great power to see clearly into himself without tergiversation, *and act thence,* will come to his destiny."

*

Courage? On the level where the only thing that counts is a man's loyalty to himself, the word has no meaning. —"Was he brave?"—"No, just logical."

*

"Watchman, what of the night? Watchman, what of the night? The watchman said, The morning cometh, and also the night." *(Isaiah 21:11–12)*

"And the Lord said, If I find in Sodom fifty righteous within the city, then I will spare all the place for their sakes. . . . Oh let not the Lord be angry, and I will speak yet but this once: Peradventure ten shall be found there. And he said, I will not destroy it for ten's sake." *(Genesis 18:26, 32)*

"But when they shall deliver you up, take no thought how or what ye shall speak: for it shall be given you in that same hour what ye shall speak. For it is not ye that speak, but the Spirit of your Father which speaketh in you." *(Matthew 10:19–20)*

*

The ultimate experience is the same for all:

"Only the most absolute sincerity under heaven can bring the inborn talent to the full and empty the chalice of the nature. He who can totally sweep clean the chalice of himself can carry the inborn nature of others to its fulfillment . . . this clarifying activity has no limit, it neither stops nor stays . . . it stands in the emptiness above with the sun, seeing and judging, interminable in space and time, searching, enduring . . . unseen it causes harmony; unmoving it transforms; unmoved it perfects." *(Tsze Sze, not Eckhart)*

*

Semina motuum. In us the creative instinct became will. In order to grow beautifully like a tree, we have to attain a peaceful self-unity in which the creative will is retransformed into instinct. —Eckhart's "habitual will."

"—looking straight into one's own heart—
    (as we can do in the mirror-image of the Father)
—watching with affection the way people grow—
    (as in imitation of the Son)
—coming to rest in perfect equity"
    (as in the fellowship of the Holy Ghost)

Like the ultimate experience, our ethical experience is the same for all. Even the Way of the Confucian world is a "Trinity."

*

With the love of Him who knows all,
With the patience of Him whose now is eternal,
With the righteousness of Him who has never
    failed,
With the humility of Him who has suffered all
    the possibilities of betrayal.

*

7.29.56
8.16.56

"I believe verily to see the goodness of the Lord in the land of the living.

O tarry thou the Lord's leisure: be strong and He shall comfort thine heart." *(Psalm 27:15,16)*

"But when you can find no consolation except in God, then, of a truth, He will console you."

"The man who possesses that light which is the Hidden God, is in a tragic situation—: he is no longer able to live by the golden mean, but must live without rest in the tension between mutually exclusive demands." . . . (Julien Gracques: *Le Rivage des Syrtes*)

"In the process of this absolute sincerity, one can arrive at a knowledge of what will occur."

❋

"I cannot go to cure the body of my patient, but I forget my profession, and call unto God for his soul." (Sir Thomas Browne: *Religio Medici*)

"We carry with us the wonders we seek without us." *(Ibid.)*

Sayings resonant with significance—to one who is seeking the Kingdom of God, they contain the truth about *all* work.

❋

8.26.56

Uneasy, uneasy, uneasy—
Why?

Because—when opportunity gives you the obligation to create, you are content to meet the demands of the moment, from one day to the next.

Because—anxious for the good opinion of others, and jealous of the possibility that they may become "famous," you have lowered yourself to wondering what will happen in the end to what you have done and been. How dead can a man be behind a façade of great ability, loyalty—and ambition! Bless your uneasiness as a sign that there is still life in you.

*

Twice now you have done him an injustice. In spite of the fact that you were "right" or, more correctly, *because* you were, in your conceit and your stupid pride in your powers you went stumping on over ground where each step gave him pain.

*

"—With Thee: in faith and courage."
No—in *self-denial*, faith and courage.

*

8.30.56

E.L.:

"To take Captivity captive."* Above all, a question of faith.

"To take Captivity captive." It is an *idea* you are serving—an idea which must be victorious if a mankind worth the name is to survive.

It is this idea which you must help towards victory with all your strength—not the work of human hands which just now gives you responsibility and the responsibility-creating chance to further it.

Knowing this, it should be easy for you to smile at criticism of decisions misunderstood, ridicule of expressions misinterpreted as "idealism," declarations of war to the death upon that to which, for all outward appearances, you are devoting your life.

But is it so easy? No—for the pettiness you show in your reactions to other people about whose motives *you* know nothing, renders you—very justly—vulnerable to the pettiness you encounter in interpretations of your own efforts.

Only on one level are you what you can be. Only in one direction are you free. Only at one point are you outside time. The good fortune of "Sunday's child" is simply this: that he meets his destiny *at* that point, *in* that direction, *on* that level.

> Two traits observed in today's mirror:
> > ambitious—not in itself, perhaps, a fault, but
> > how short the step to pride or self-pity!
> > joyless—and a killer of joy.

*

---

* The initials stand for Erik Lindegren, the Swedish poet, who in a letter to H. used the phrase "to capture death." The aptest English equivalent I could think of was the phrase I have quoted from *The Book of Common Prayer*, which continues . . . *and tread down Satan under our feet.* W. H. A.

118

In the suction of the vacuum, created when a strain upon the nerves ceases but the nerves have not yet relaxed, the lust of the flesh gets its chance to reveal the loneliness of the soul.

*

The "men of the hour," the self-assured who strut about among us in the jingling harness of their success and importance, how can you let yourself be irritated by them. Let them enjoy their triumph—on the level to which it belongs.

*

Living submerged in this heavy *Fluidum* of the sub-human—sub-human in insight, feeling, and energy—beware of a twofold danger—of drowning and of floating—of lowering yourself until this position below the clear surface of the truly human seems to you the natural one, and of upholding your banner in a vacuum of "superiority."

The fact is that, in this position, "love and patience, righteousness and humility," are necessary even for your own peace and comfort.

*

11.1–7.56

"I will lay me down in peace, and take my rest: for it is thou, Lord, only, that makest me dwell in safety." *(Psalm 4:9)*

"Hold thee still in the Lord . . . fret not thyself, else shalt thou be moved to evil." *(Psalm 37:7, 8)*

*

Every hour
Eye to eye
With this love
Which sees all
But overlooks
In patience,
Which is justice,
But does not condemn
If our glances
Mirror its own
In humility.

*

It was when Lucifer first congratulated himself upon his angelic behavior that he became the tool of evil.

*

Without our being aware of it, our fingers are so guided that a pattern is created when the thread gets caught in the web.

*

11.17.56

My devise—if any:
  Numen semper adest.
  In that case: if uneasy—why?

*

How humble the tool when praised for what the hand has done.

*

From injustice—never justice.
From justice—never injustice.

*

Somebody placed the shuttle in your hand: somebody who had already arranged the threads.

*

11.25.56

> If you give all, but life retain,
> Your gift is nothing and in vain.
> (Ibsen: Brand)

*

11.29.56

Faulkner: Our final wish is to have scribbled on the wall our "Kilroy was here."

The last ditch of the enemy. We can sacrifice ourselves completely to that which is beyond and above us—and *still* hope that the memory of our choice shall remain tied to our name or, at least, that future generations shall understand why and how we acted. At times it seems to us that the bitterness we feel when we fail at an attempted task lies in this: that our failure will condemn our efforts themselves to oblivion.

O contradiction! O last stand! If only the goal can justify the sacrifice, how, then, can you attach a shadow of importance to the question whether or not the memory of your efforts will be associated with your name? If you do, is it not all too obvious that you are still being influenced in your actions by that vain dead dream about "posterity"?

*

The question answered itself:
"I believe that we should die with decency so that at least decency will survive."

*

Hallowed be Thy name,
not mine,
Thy kingdom come,
not mine,
Thy will be done,
not mine,
Give us peace with Thee
Peace with men
Peace with ourselves,
And free us from all fear.

※

"He brought me forth also into a place of liberty: he brought me forth, even because he had a favor unto me.

"The Lord did reward me after my righteous dealing: according to the cleanness of my hands did he recompense me." *(Psalm 18:20–21)*

And again:

"For there is mercy with thee: therefore shalt thou be feared." *(Psalm 130:4)*

※

12.24.56

Your own efforts "did not bring it to pass," only God —but rejoice if God found a use for your efforts in His work.

Rejoice if you feel that what you did was "necessary," but remember, even so, that you were simply the instrument by means of which He added one tiny grain to the Universe He has created for His own purposes.

"It is in this abyss that you reveal me to myself—I am nothing and I did not know it.

"If, without any side glances, we have only God in view, it is He, indeed, who does what we do.... Such a man does not seek rest, for he is not troubled by any unrest. . . . He must acquire an inner solitude, no matter where or with whom he may be: he must learn to pierce the veil of things and comprehend God *within them.*" *(Meister Eckhart)*

✳

12.25.56

"Of the Eternal Birth"—to me, this now says everything there is to be said about what I have learned and have still to learn.

"The soul that would experience this birth must detach herself from all outward things: within herself completely at one with herself. . . . You must have an exalted mind and a *burning* heart in which, nevertheless, reign silence and stillness." *(Meister Eckhart)*

✳

12.26.56

"It merely happens to one man and not to others . . . but he can take no credit to himself for the gifts and the responsibility assigned to him . . . destiny is something not to be desired and not to be avoided . . . it is a mystery not contrary to reason, for it implies that the world, and the course of human history, have meaning."

✳

Vanity rears its ridiculous little head and holds up the distorting mirror in front of you. For an instant, the play actor adjusts his smile and his features to the role. For a mere instant—but one too many. It is at such times that you invite defeat and betray Him whom you serve.

✳

You ask yourself if these notes are not, after all, false to the very Way they are intended to mark.

These notes?—They were signposts you began to set up after you had reached a point where you needed them, a fixed point that was on no account to be lost sight of. And so they have remained. But your life has changed, and now you reckon with possible readers, even, perhaps, hope for them. Still, perhaps it may be of interest to somebody to learn about a path about which the traveler who was committed to it did not wish to speak while he was alive. Perhaps—but only if what you write has an honesty with no trace of vanity or self-regard.

*

Forward! Thy orders are given in secret. May I always hear them—and obey.

Forward! Whatever distance I have covered, it does not give me the right to halt.

Forward! It is the attention given to the last steps before the summit which decides the value of all that went before.

*

We act in faith—and miracles occur. In consequence, we are tempted to make the miracles the ground for our faith. The cost of such weakness is that we lose the confidence of faith. Faith *is,* faith creates, faith carries. It is not derived from, nor created, nor carried by anything except its own reality.

*

12.31.56

"In the volume of the book it is written of me, that I should fulfill thy will, O my God: I am content to do it; yea, thy Law is within my heart.

I have declared thy righteousness in the great congregation: lo, I will not refrain my lips, O Lord, and that thou knowest." *(Psalm 40:10–11)*

*

Your confidence was very slight. So much the more must you now abase yourself when, in spite of this, it has come to pass according to your faith.

*

Gratitude and readiness. You got all for nothing. Do not hesitate, when it is asked for, to give your all, which, in fact, is nothing, for all.

*

Be grateful as your deeds become less and less associated with your name, as your feet ever more lightly tread the earth.

1957

Night is drawing nigh—

Each day the first day: each day a life.

Each morning we must hold out the chalice of our being to receive, to carry, and give back. It must be held out empty—for the past must only be reflected in its polish, its shape, its capacity.

. . . and those things which for our unworthiness we dare not, and for our blindness we cannot ask, vouchsafe to give us. . . .

(*The Book of Common Prayer,* General Collect)

*

The most dangerous of all moral dilemmas: when we are obliged to conceal truth in order to help the truth to be victorious. If this should at any time become our duty in the role assigned us by fate, how strait must be our path at all times if we are not to perish.

*

You saved him from victory and, after his defeat, showed him kindness out of a *Schadenfreude* you sorely needed to indulge in. You have, indeed, earned the right to a sympathetic audience.

❋

Did the attack hurt you—in spite of its absurdity—because it made you feel ridiculous when the leading role was assigned to a little bank clerk?* Would it have hurt, though, if the little bank clerk had not begun to fancy himself as a bit of a hero?

—Not I, but God in me!

❋

1.21.57

Destruction! What fury in your attack, how cruel your victory over this poor old body! You razed everything, you plunged a mind into abysses of anguish—and released this smile of ultimate joy.

❋

2.24.57

We can reach the point where it becomes possible for us to recognize and understand Original Sin, that dark counter-center of evil in our nature—that is to say, though it *is* not our nature, it is *of* it—that something within us which rejoices when disaster befalls the very cause we are trying to serve, or misfortune overtakes even those whom we love.

Life in God is not an escape from this, but the way to gain full insight concerning it. It is not our depravity which forces a fictitious religious explanation upon us,

---

*H. has Pinneberg, a reference to Hans Fallada's novel *Little Man, What Now,* but I could not think of any equivalent in British or in American novels. W. H. A.

but the experience of religious reality which forces the "Night Side" out into the light.

It is when we stand in the righteous all-seeing light of love that we can dare to look at, admit, and *consciously* suffer under this something in us which wills disaster, misfortune, defeat to everything outside the sphere of our narrowest self-interest. So a living relation to God is the necessary precondition for the self-knowledge which enables us to follow a straight path, and so be victorious over ourselves, forgiven by ourselves.

*

Oedipus, the son of a king, the winner of a throne, fortunate and innocent, is compelled to recognize the possibility and, in the end, the fact that he, too, is guilty, which makes it just that he should be sacrificed to save the city.

*

Success—for the glory of God or for your own, for the peace of mankind or for your own? Upon the answer to this question depends the result of your actions.

*

4.7.57

How am I to find the strength to live as a free man, detached from all that was unjust in my past and all that is petty in my present, and so, daily, to forgive myself?

Life will judge me by the measure of the love *I myself* am capable of, and with patience according to the measure of my honesty in attempting to meet its demands, and with an equity before which the feeble explanations and excuses of self-importance carry no weight whatsoever.

＊

What has Life lost by the happiness which might have been his, had he been allowed to go on living? What has it gained by the suffering he has escaped?

What nonsense I'm talking! Life is measured by the living, and the number of a man's days are reckoned in other terms.

＊

Not to brood over my pettiness with masochistic self-disgust, nor to take a pride in admitting it—but to recognize it as a threat to my integrity of action, the moment I let it out of my sight.

＊

How selfish and aesthetic our so-called "sympathy" usually is. There come times when, momentarily, we can serve as the foundation for somebody else's faith in himself—a faith which is constantly being threatened in all of us. When this happens, what we do to make it possible for him to "go on," we make the foundation for our own life-preserving self-esteem.

In this matter—as in many others—realism is the opposite of desecration. The truth we have to endure is our present reality without the justifications which time may provide.

*

For the sacrificed—in the hour of sacrifice—only one thing counts: faith—alone among enemies and skeptics. Faith, in spite of the humiliation which is both the necessary precondition and the consequence of faith, faith without any hope of compensation other than he can find in a faith which reality seems so thoroughly to refute.

Would the Crucifixion have had any sublimity or meaning if Jesus had seen Himself crowned with the halo of martyrdom? What we have later added was not there for Him. And we must forget all about it if we are to hear His commands.

*

We have to acquire a peace and balance of mind such that we can give every word of criticism its due weight, and humble ourselves before every word of praise.

*

4.28.57

There is no history but that of the soul, no peace but that of the soul. *(St.-John Perse)*

*

Clad in this "self," the creation of irresponsible and ignorant persons, meaningless honors and catalogued acts—strapped into the strait jacket of the immediate.

To step out of all this, and stand naked on the precipice of dawn—acceptable, invulnerable, free: in the Light, with the Light, of the Light. *Whole,* real in the Whole.

Out of myself as a stumbling block, into myself as fulfillment.

*

5.25.57

"Why," you ask, "deny yourself something which does nobody else any harm and does you good?"

Yes, why—provided it does not conflict with the path you have chosen. Your subsequent reaction to your behavior when you have forgotten this proviso—as one reacts to a lie or a humiliating weakness—is sufficient answer to your question.

*

Everything in the present moment, nothing for the present moment. And nothing for your future comfort or the future of your good name.

*

Suddenly—without your help—some impasse or other you have dared your all to break, disappears. But you are tempted to "keep yourself well to the fore"—whether this helps the cause or doesn't—even, perhaps, without caring if it might do harm.

Do you wish to forfeit even that little to which your efforts may have entitled you? Only if your endeavors are inspired by a devotion to duty in which you forget yourself completely, can you keep your faith in their value.

This being so, your endeavor to reach the goal should have taught you to rejoice when others reach it.

*

6.20.57

"—a lie or a humiliating weakness—" One consequence among others: you suffer under criticism which is *not* justified. Yes, and let it sap your strength to meet your task.

6.23.57

"For he maketh the storm to cease: so that the waves thereof are still.

Then are they glad, because they are at rest: and so he bringeth them unto the haven where they would be." *(Psalm 107:29–30)*

*

"The flutes of exile." *(St.-John Perse)* Forever among strangers to all that has shaped your life—*alone*. Forever thirsting for the living waters—but not even free to seek them, a *prisoner*.

The answer—the hard straight brutal answer: in the One you are never alone, in the One you are always at home.

*

Result and reaction— The intense blaze of your anxiety reveals to what a great extent you are still fettered, still alienated from the One.

However, don't worry about this or anything else, but follow the Way of which you are aware, even when you have departed from it.

"Nevertheless, not as I will, but as Thou wilt."

*

He who is challenged by Fate does not take umbrage at the terms.

*

For someone whose job so obviously mirrors man's extraordinary possibilities and responsibilities, there is no excuse if he loses his sense of "having been called." So long as he keeps that, everything he can do has a meaning, nothing a price. Therefore: if he complains, he is accusing—himself.

*

The myths have always condemned those who "looked back." Condemned them, whatever the paradise may have been which they were leaving. Hence this shadow over each departure from your decision, "O traveller towards the Dawn." (*Hermann Hesse*)

*

7.20.57

False—furtive. When shut out of the room, you must not peep through the keyhole. Either break down the door, or go away.

False—furtive. Only among people to whom the truth would have seemed a denial of your choice. Nevertheless, whatever your reasons for concealment, so long as you feel ashamed, it may, in spite of everything, turn out for the good.

*

7.28.57

You are not the oil, you are not the air—merely the point of combustion, the flash-point where the light is born.

You are merely the lens in the beam. You can only receive, give, and possess the light as a lens does.

If you seek yourself, "your rights," you prevent the oil and air from meeting in the flame, you rob the lens of its transparency. Sanctity—either to be the Light, or to be self-effaced in the Light, so that it may be born, self-effaced so that it may be focused or spread wider.

*

You will know Life and be acknowledged by it according to your degree of transparency, your capacity, that is, to vanish as an end, and remain purely as a means.

*

9.3.57

"To forgive oneself"—? No, that doesn't work: we have to *be forgiven*. But we can only believe this is possible if we ourselves can forgive.

✳

Your responsibility is indeed terrifying. If you fail, it is God, thanks to your having betrayed Him, who will fail mankind. You fancy you can be responsible *to* God; can you carry the responsibility *for* God?

✳

"To fail"— Are you satisfied because you have curbed and canalized the worst in you? In any human situation, it is cheating not to *be*, at every moment, one's best. How much more so in a position where others have faith in you.

✳

9.26.57

"The best and most wonderful thing that can happen to you in this life, is that you should be silent and let God work and speak."

Long ago, you gripped me, Slinger. *Now* into the storm. *Now* towards your target.

✳

10.1.57

> It whispers: all is waiting here,
> Kept safe for thee, year after year,
> Beautiful songs in thousands;
> Where hast thou been. where, where?
> *(Erik Axel Karlfeldt)*

*

Do not look back. And do not dream about the future, either. It will neither give you back the past, nor satisfy your other daydreams. Your duty, your reward—your destiny—are *here* and *now*.

*

Jesus' "lack of moral principles." He sat at meat with publicans and sinners, he consorted with harlots. Did he do this to obtain their votes? Or did he think that, perhaps, he could convert them by such "appeasement"? Or was his humanity rich and deep enough to make contact, even in them, with that in human nature which is common to all men, indestructible, and upon which the future has to be built?

*

10.6.57

Yes to God: yes to Fate: yes to yourself. This reality can wound the soul, but has the power to heal her.
> "Endless the series of things without name
> On the way back to where there is nothing."

*

Another opportunity was given you—as a favor and as a burden. The question is not: why did it happen this way, or where is it going to lead you, or what is the price you will have to pay. It is simply: *how* are you making use of it. And about that there is only *one* who can judge.

*

You told yourself you would accept the decision of fate. But you lost your nerve when you discovered what this would require of you: then you realized how attached you still were to the world which has made you what you were, but which you would now have to leave behind. It felt like an amputation, a "little death," and you even listened to those voices which insinuated that you were deceiving yourself out of ambition. You will have to give up everything. Why, then, weep at this little death? Take it to you—quickly—with a smile die this death, and become free to go further—one with your task, whole in your duty of the moment.

*

You have not done enough, you have never done enough, so long as it is still possible that you have something of value to contribute.

This is the answer when you are groaning under what you consider a burden and an uncertainty prolonged ad infinitum.

*

"The Uncarved Block"—remain at the Center, which is yours and that of all humanity. For those goals which it gives to your life, do the utmost which, at each moment, is possible for you. Also, act without thinking of the consequences, or seeking anything for yourself.

*

Do not seek death. Death will find you. But seek the road which makes death a fulfillment.

*

Your body must become familiar with its death—in all its possible forms and degrees—as a self-evident, imminent, and emotionally neutral step on the way towards the goal you have found worthy of your life.

*

As an element in the sacrifice, death is a fulfillment, but more often it is a degradation, and it is never an elevation.

*

The *arête* that leads to the summit separates two abysses: the pleasure-tinged death wish (not, perhaps, without an element of narcissistic masochism), and the animal fear arising from the physical instinct for survival. Only he can conquer vertigo, whose body has learned to treat itself as a means.

*

No choice is uninfluenced by the way in which the personality regards its destiny, and the body its death. In the last analysis, it is our conception of death which decides our answers to all the questions that life puts to us. That is why it requires its proper place and time —if need be, with right of precedence. Hence, too, the necessity of preparing for it.

*

Courage and love: equivalent and related expressions for your bargain with Life. You are willing to "pay" what your heart commands you to give. Two associated reflexes to the sacrificial act, conditioned by a self-chosen effacement of the personality in the One. One result of "God's marriage to the Soul" is a union with other people which does not draw back before the ultimate surrender of the self.

*

Did you choose your words carefully enough, what impression did you make, did they think you were trying to be ingratiating, etc.? It is questions like these which keep you awake. Are you no longer confident that your instinctive reactions will guide you right? If so, you know why. You have allowed your hunger for "justice" to make you self-conscious, so that, in the performance of your task, you no longer forget yourself. So, and only so, can you be wounded by the opinions of the crowd.

*

Praise those of your critics for whom nothing is up to standard.

*

In play, the body can learn the model for actions in real life. Its lust can prepare a man to endure tribulation.

*

12.22.57

The madman shouted in the market place. No one stopped to answer him. Thus it was confirmed that his thesis was incontrovertible.

*

12.24.57

In Thy wind—in Thy light—
How insignificant is everything else, how small are we—and how happy in that which alone is great.

1958

————▪—▪—▪—————

So shall the world be created each morning anew, *for-given*—in Thee, by Thee.

*

2.16.58

"—shew the light of thy countenance; and we shall be whole." *(Psalm 80:19)*

"Believe me: this, too, belongs to perfection, that a man so undertakes works, that all his works fuse into one work. This must be done 'in the Kingdom of God.' For I tell you the truth: all works which man does out-side of the Kingdom of God are dead, but those which he does in the Kingdom of God are alive . . . just as God is not distracted or changed by any of his works, nor, too, is the soul so long as she works according to the law of God's kingdom. Such men, therefore, may do works or do them not, but remain all the while undisturbed. *For works neither give them anything, nor take anything from them.*" *(Meister Eckhart)*

*

"In the Kingdom of God— ; —all works are equal there, my smallest is as my greatest, my greatest as my smallest. —About works in themselves there is something divisive which causes a division in the souls of men, and brings them to the brink of disquiet." *(Meister Eckhart)*

*

"After the fireworks"; how much simpler life is, how much more difficult, how much *purer,* and how much more terrifying.

*

That piece of pagan anthropomorphism: the belief that, in order to educate us, God wishes us to suffer. How far from this is the assent to suffering when it strikes us *because* we have obeyed what we have seen to be God's will.

*

The pure, simple self at the hour of waking—and the first thing it sees—its grotesque image in the distorting mirror of yesterday.

*

4.10.58

In the faith which is "God's marriage to the soul," you are *one* in God, and
>God is wholly in you,
>just as, for you, He is wholly in all you meet.

With this faith, in prayer you descend into yourself to meet the Other,
>in the steadfastness and light of this union,
>see that all things stand, like yourself, alone before God,
>and that each of your acts is an act of creation, conscious, because you are a human being with human responsibility, but governed, nevertheless, by the power beyond human consciousness which has created man.

You are liberated from things, but you encounter in them an experience which has the purity and clarity of revelation.

In the faith which is "God's marriage to the soul," *everything*, therefore, has a meaning.

So live, then, that you may use what has been put into your hand. . . .

*

Only in man has the evolution of the creation reached the point where reality encounters itself in judgment and choice. Outside of man, the creation is neither good nor evil.

Only when you descend into yourself and encounter the Other, do you then experience goodness as the ultimate reality—united and living—*in* Him and *through* you.

*

7.29.58

Did'st Thou give me this inescapable loneliness so that it would be easier for me to give Thee all?

*

Still a few years more, and then? The only value of a life is its content—for *others*. Apart from any value it may have for others, my life is worse than death. Therefore, in my great loneliness, serve others. Therefore: how incredibly great is what I have been given, and how meaningless what I have to "sacrifice."

> Hallowed be Thy Name,
> Thy kingdom come,
> Thy will be done—

*

You wake from dreams of doom and—for a moment—you *know:* beyond all the noise and the gestures, the only real thing, love's calm unwavering flame in the half-light of an early dawn.

*

The fire of the body
burns away its dross and, rising in a flame of self-surrender, consumes its closed microcosm.

*

The ultimate surrender to the creative act—it is the destiny of some to be brought to the threshold of this in the act of sacrifice rather than the sexual act; and they experience a thunderclap of the same dazzling power.

10.5.58

Fading beeches, bright against*
A dark storm-cloud.
Wind rips up the forest-pond's
Steel-gray water.
On the earth between bloodstains
The tracks of deer.

Silence shatters to pieces
The mind's armor,
Leaving it naked before
Autumn's clear eye.

---

* In Swedish verse it is not the convention, I am told, to capitalize the initial letter of each line. After some hesitation, I decided to conform to English practice.

Except when writing free verse, H. orders his verses by syllabic count, and I have tried, whenever possible, to make my versions conform to the syllabic counting of the originals. W. H. A.

The mine-detector
Weaves its old pattern
Without end.

Words without import
Are lobbed to and fro
Between us.

Forgotten intrigues
With their spider's web
Snare our hands.

Choked by its clown's mask
And quite dry, my mind
Is crumbling.

10.12.58

Day slowly bleeds to death
Through the wound made
When the sharp horizon's edge
Ripped through the sky.
Into its now empty veins
Seeps the darkness.
The corpse stiffens,
Embraced by the chill of night.

Over the dead one are lit
Some silent stars.

Lord—Thine the day,
And I the day's.

SINGLE FORM*

The breaking wave
And the muscle as it contracts
Obey the same law.

An austere line
Gathers the body's play of strength
In a bold balance.

Shall my soul meet
This curve, as a bend in the road
On her way to form?

---

* The title of a piece of sculpture by Barbara Hepworth. The syllabic count of the original stanza is 6.6.5. W. H. A.

10.19.58

Too tired for company,
You seek a solitude
You are too tired to fill.

*

Wall of power
In assault,
Wave of light
In the pause,
Then broken,
Receding
From the lip
Of white sand,
Foam and froth.

1959

———

2.8.59

"But lo, thou requirest truth in the inward parts: and shall make me to understand wisdom secretly." *(Psalm 51:6)*

In "faith"—an unbroken living contact with all things. "Before God," therefore the soul is in the truth.

*

Conscious of the reality of evil and the tragedy of the individual life, and conscious, too, of the demand that life be conducted with decency.

*

2.9.59

What distinguishes the "elite" from the masses is only their insistence upon "quality." This implies a responsibility, to all for all, to the past for the future, which is the reflection of a humble and spontaneous response to Life—with its endless possibilities, and its unique present which never happens twice.

*

7.29.59

Humility is just as much the opposite of self-abasement as it is of self-exaltation. To be humble is *not to make comparisons*. Secure in its reality, the self is neither better nor worse, bigger nor smaller, than anything else in the universe. It *is*—is nothing, yet at the same time one with everything. It is in this sense that humility is absolute self-effacement.

To be nothing in the self-effacement of humility, yet, for the sake of the task, to embody *its* whole weight and importance in your bearing, as the one who has been called to undertake it. To give to people, works, poetry, art, what the self can contribute, and to take, simply and freely, what belongs to it by reason of its identity. Praise and blame, the winds of success and adversity, blow over such a life without leaving a trace or upsetting its balance.

Towards this, so help me, God—

*

8.4.59

To have humility is to experience reality, not *in relation to ourselves,* but in its sacred independence. It is to see, judge, and act from the point of rest in ourselves. Then, how much disappears, and all that remains falls into place.

In the point of rest at the center of our being, we encounter a world where all things are at rest in the same way. Then a tree becomes a mystery, a cloud a revelation, each man a cosmos of whose riches we can only catch glimpses. The life of simplicity is simple, but it opens to us a book in which we never get beyond the first syllable.

8.4.59

> *Seventeen syllables**
> *Opened the door*
> *To memory, to meaning.*

*

FROM UPPSALA

8.7.59

Red evenings in March. News of death.
Begin anew—
What has ended?

Night. Plains. An empty hall.
In the window niche
She waits for the sunrise.

Cockchafers. Sorb-apple blossom.
Lilacs conversing
After bedtime.

The trees pant. Silence.
An irresolute raindrop furrows
The dark pane.

---

* In a haiku, the number of syllables in any one line is optional,
but the sum total of the three lines must always be seventeen. In my
English versions, the number of syllables in any given line may not
be the same as in the Swedish, but the total for the three is the
same. W. H. A.

A cone of light in the fog.
A winter moth dancing
Round the lamp post.

Gray snow-walls. Warm horse-dung.
The houses stretch themselves,
Stale in the morning.

8.9.59

The plain's horizon,
The wall's vertical,
Intersect like two fate-lines.

Swollen brooks
Under Easter skies.
Night. On the table sweet violets.

In the Stone Age night
A church spire, erect on the plain
Like a phallus.

Dawn in the east. From the wide plain
Blue sacrificial smokes
Go straight up.

The boy in the forest
Throws off his best Sunday suit
And plays naked.

The fountain plays.
Among white peonies
The digger wasp goes hunting.

Black shooting stars,
The swallows utter shrill cries
As they mate in mid-air.

In the bare poplar a voice
Of such well-being
It burst space open.

The Easter lily's dew-wet calyx.
Drops pausing
Between earth and sky.

New leaves at sunset
After May showers. A look back
Repeats the Fall.

Flytrap, dog rose.
The hedgehog keeps his watch
About the sleeping castle.

Dead pools in quarries.
On the scrubby heath
Swarms of peacock butterflies.

In the shadow of the castle
The flowers closed
Long before nightfall.

The castle saw them,
Filming Charles the Twelfth
In a gray blizzard.

Smell of bread. Homely words.
The light faded
In the snow's whirling ashes.

More than years stood between them
On their night tour
Of deserted alleys.

On that New Year's Eve
The black shadows of elms
Gave shelter to the graves.

Ten years ripening.
Ten years waiting.
Soon: twenty long years in the earth.

Arzareth's morning light.*
Long spring evenings
Which looked for a meaning.

He lowered his eyes,
Lest he should see the body
To lust after it.

---

* "Through that region there was a long way to go, a journey of
a year and a half, and that country is called Arzareth." *(2 Esdras
13:45)*

"And the Lord rooted them out of their land in anger, and in
wrath, and in great indignation, and cast them into another land, as
it is this day." *(Deuteronomy 29:28)*

My home drove me
Into the wilderness.
Few look for me. Few hear me.

Denied the Sought-After,
He longed to deserve
To be the Sought-After.

A box on the ear taught the boy
That Father's name
Was odious to them.

He fell when he tried to vault.
They all had their laugh
At such a sissy.

His moral lecture
Blazed with hate.
What could have driven a child that far?

They laid the blame on him.
He didn't know what it was,
But he confessed it.

He wasn't wanted.
When, nonetheless, he came,
He could only watch them play.

School was over. The yard was empty.
The ones he sought
Had found new friends.

Honeysuckle.
In a gray twilight
His sensuality awoke.

By the lilac hedge
With no "duties,"
She was back in the Land of Youth.

The winter twilight grays
Beyond the pane.
The caged bird's breast is bleeding.

Her parcels fell in the mud,
But she dismissed the mishap
With a smile.

Morning, clear as a spring,
Rouses to life
The butterfly cotillions.

You will never return.
Another man
Will find another homestead.

SUMMERS

Crowberry tickles the neck.
Above the blue abyss
Floats a buzzard.

Gray lichens. Red berries.
Harp string plucked on the shore.
Hush! The diver sleeps.

He found a new ranunculus.
No smarter than we,
He went further.

Fragrance of linden trees. Twilight.
We dreamed of finding
A Death's-Head Moth.

The leaf mould under the alders
Hid from us
The secrets of Orchis.

In the copse a slab
For human sacrifice
To placate the sea wind.

Cuckoo west, cuckoo best.
Her husband is dead
And her two cows are sold.

First piping of northern warblers
Over white ice fields.
Space is thawing.

White glacier crow's-foot,
Alone among the stones.
Frost where the shadow falls.

The glow in the windows died.
The gate was shut.
Lark song. Quiver of wings.

Years of pilgrimage—ahead, the East—
At the dark stream
Under the lindens.

The quay. Clatter of steps.
Glitter. Gulls shrieked.
An innocent day was born.

Midge dance. Blast-furnace smoke.
Adder asleep
Near the wild strawberry patch.

Thunder-still rooms.
Roar of rapids round the ait
Where he looked for tansies.

Lightning struck.
Heads of the Firm stepped down
From the Limbo of their portraits.

Steep Swedish hills.
The coachman in front
Flicked the horse's sweating crupper.

FAR AWAY

The brilliant notes of the flute
Are heard by the gods
In the Cave of Birth.

Himalayan ice cliffs*
Beyond the hills
Of Vezelay† at Easter.

Apes. The moon woke them—
Round the world's navel revolved
Prayer wheels of steps.

A place of rest. Charcoal fires.
Deep in the mirror
Vishnu is at peace.

---

* This haiku and the two which follow it are based on H.'s visit
to the Buddhist shrine of Swayambhunath, outside Katmandu in
Nepal. See H.'s own account in "A New Look at Everest" (*National
Geographic Magazine*, January 1961). W. H. A.

† A village on the banks of the river Cure in the department of
Yonne, famous for its basilica, the Madeleine. During the years
when H. was working in Paris, he used often to visit it. W. H. A.

On Christmas Eve, Good Friday
Was foretold them
In a trumpet fanfare.

Sough of palm and beat of wave
Joined in the anthem
From the land of snow.

Orgasms of bodies
On hot nights, lit
By flickers of summer lightning.

With a thrill of desire
His body sank, sun-drenched,
Into the salt wave.

HUDSON VALLEY

A warm autumn night. A moon
Lighting this path—
Far away a heart stops.

A verandah in the forest,
A thousand bow-strokes,
Brief light-signals.

April snow.
The cardinal sought shelter
In the white forsythia.

The belly the car slit open
Was silent
When borne to the roadside.

Trees quiver in the wind,
Sailing on a sea of mist
Out of earshot.

At my whistle
She came out of the birdhouse,
Turned back disappointed.

Your body, your mind
—In trust—like the baton
Borne in a relay race.

When he saw them all flee,
The skunk decided
He was the King of Beasts.

On the drawing-room table
The book became soiled,
And the text was lost.

When the gods play,
They look for a string
That has never been touched by men.

9.13.59

May I be offered
To that in the offering
Which will be offered.

God took the form of man
In the victim
Who chose to be sacrificed.

Denied any outlet,
The heat transmuted
The coal into diamonds.

Beauty, Goodness,
In the wonder's here and now
Became suddenly real.

Not knowing the question,
It was easy for him
To give the answer.

Do you create?
Or destroy? *That's*
For your ordeal-by-fire to answer.

The cicadas shrieked
As the glowing sky consumed
Their last evening.

Up there, in the cold empty spaces,
Nebulae of starlings
Whirl by.

Trees, waters, crescent moon—
All things tonight
In shivering osmosis.

Congenial to other people?
It is with yourself
That you must live.

He fell from the rock ledge
When, too scared to walk upright,
He tried to crawl.

Grass wet from rain:
His bare feet tried to find
Their seedbed in the humus.

Alone in his secret growth,
He found a kinship
With all growing things.

When he interprets
What he wished to forget,
He speaks to the future.
                    (Paul La Cour*)

One in our bodies'
Vow to transcend
The physically possible.
                    (T. E. Lawrence)

On the coast of Barbary
This grim fort
For the Queen of Heaven.

10.25.59

That chapter is closed.
Nothing binds me:
All is made ready, all waiting.

Wherever we may hide ourselves,
Still this salt spray
From a sun-lit surf.

---

* Danish poet (1902–1956).   W. H. A.

Far inland,
The freshness of the sea still played
Among leaves of bright bronze.

Because it never found a mate,
Men called
The unicorn abnormal.

11.1.59

Doffing the ego's
Safe glory, he finds
His naked reality.
                    (O'Neill: *Billy Brown*)

He gave his life
For the happiness of others,
But wished them evil.

What the shaving satyr
In the mirror mocked at,
He bought with his life.

Let them keep
All the petty secrets
They have guarded so anxiously.

This accidental
Meeting of possibilities
Calls itself *I*.

I ask: what am I doing here?
And, at once, this *I*
Becomes unreal.

This morning,
The singing of the birds filled his mind
With the night's cool peace.

The words did not exist
Which should have captured
His desire and terror.

The book remained shut—
Naked, I saw
The naked instruments of death.

The goldenrod stirs:
Milkwort's white parachute
Is opened by the wind.

Like dishonest farm bailiffs,
We squander
His wealth for our salvation.

A sky as blue
As that above the snow-crest
Before the last ski-run.
                    (Gösta Lundqvist*)

While the shots echoed,
For the sake of Life
He sought the living word.

Be pure and dare—
In this fight with the mountain,
With myself against me.

No cracking of the whip of words
Disturbed his peace
In a space that sang.

For him who has faith,
The last miracle
Shall be greater than the first.

---

* Photographer and, like H., a member of the Swedish Alpine
Club. W. H. A.

1960

—§—§—§—

Easter, 1960

Forgiveness breaks the chain of causality because he who "forgives" you—out of love—takes upon himself the consequences of what *you* have done. Forgiveness, therefore, always entails a sacrifice.

The price you must pay for your own liberation through another's sacrifice is that you in turn must be willing to liberate in the same way, irrespective of the consequences to yourself.

*

When I think of those who have preceded me, I feel as if I were at a party in the dead hour which has to be got through after the Guests of Honor have left.

When I think of those who will come after—or survive me—I feel as if I were taking part in the preparations for a feast, the joys of which I shall not share.

*

173

Christmas Eve, 1960

How proper it is that Christmas should follow Advent.
—For him who looks towards the future, the Manger
is situated on Golgotha, and the Cross has already been
raised in Bethlehem.

> Strive, the pains of death endure,
> Peace eternal to secure:
> For the faithful and the tried
> Heaven's Gates shall open wide.
> *(Archbishop J. O. Wallin, 1819)*

"I will lay me down in peace, and take my rest; for it
is thou, Lord, only that makest me dwell in safety."
(Psalm 4:9)
"Thou hast showed thy people heavy things: thou hast
given us a drink of deadly wine.

Thou hast given a token for such as fear thee: that
they may triumph because of the truth." *(Psalm 60:3–4)*

The moon was caught in the branches:
Bound by its vow,
My heart was heavy.

Naked against the night
The trees slept. "Nevertheless,
Not as I will. . . ."

The burden remained mine:
They could not hear my call,
And all was silence.

Soon, now, the torches, the kiss:
Soon the gray of dawn
In the Judgment Hall.

What will their love help there?
There, the question is only
If I love them.

November 26, 1960

The tension increased.
In the noonday heat
Their wills began to waver.

Night flared.
Phosphorescent,
The jungle wailed in the fierce grip of the storm.

They paid
The full price of love
That others might enjoy a victory.

Morning mist,
Chirping of early birds.
Who recalled the night's sacrifice?

December 2, 1960

The road,
You shall follow it.

The fun,
You shall forget it.

The cup,
You shall empty it.

The pain,
You shall conceal it.

The truth,
You shall be told it.

The end,
You shall endure it.*

December 3, 1960

---

* The only rhymed poem H. wrote. Since I found myself unable
to rhyme my English version, here is the original.

> Vägen,
> du skall följa den.
>
> Lyckan,
> du skall glömma den.
>
> Kalken,
> du skall tömma den.
>
> Smärtan,
> du skall dölja den.
>
> Svaret,
> du skall lära det.
>
> Slutet,
> du skall bära det.

W. H. A.

1961

---✳✳---✳✳---✳✳---✳✳---

February 13–March 13, 1961

Thou who hast brought us to this naked life of the soul,
      Thou who broodest
On the face of the waters, wilt Thou, some evening on
      earth, relate
The tale of the hand that wraps us in the burning shirt
      of Nessus?

                  (St.-John Perse)*

✳

Be not your own pathetic fallacy, but be
Your own dark measure in the vein,
For we're about a tragic business ...
           (Djuna Barnes: *The Antiphon*)†

✳

---

* H. quotes from his own translation into Swedish. W. H. A.
 † H. quotes here in Swedish from the translation of Djuna Barnes
done by Karl Ragnar Gierow and Hammarskjöld. W. H. A.

"I became also a reproach unto them:
they that looked upon me shaked their heads.
Help me, O Lord my God:
O save me according to Thy mercy."

(Psalm 109:24–25)

*

Maundy Thursday, 1961

BRAND *(his face lifted up towards the descending avalanche):*
> The jaws of death encompass me.
> God above!
> Does it all count for nought with Thee
> That man in anguish strives to be?

(The avalanche sweeps him away. The valley is buried in snow. Through the roar a Voice is heard.)
VOICE: God is love.

(Ibsen: *Brand*)*

*

"Then thought I to understand this:
But it was too hard for me;
Until I went into the sanctuary of God."

(Psalm 73:16–17)

---

* My translation, overly free, I fear, of the last four lines of the play. H. only quotes the last three and omits the stage directions. Since I doubt if *Brand* is as familiar to the average English or American reader as it is to any Scandinavian, I felt I should be more explicit. The original lines run thus:

> Svar mig Gud i dödens slug!—
> Gjelder ej et Frelsens Fnug
> Mandeviljens *Quantum Satis?*
> —Han er *Deus Caritatis.*

W. H. A.

Whitsunday, 1961

I don't know Who—or what—put the question, I don't know when it was put. I don't even remember answering. But at some moment I did answer *Yes* to Someone —or Something—and from that hour I was certain that existence is meaningful and that, therefore, my life, in self-surrender, had a goal.

From that moment I have known what it means "not to look back," and "To take no thought for the morrow."

Led by the Ariadne's thread of my answer through the labyrinth of Life, I came to a time and place where I realized that the Way leads to a triumph which is a catastrophe, and to a catastrophe which is a triumph, that the price for committing one's life would be reproach, and that the only elevation possible to man lies in the depths of humiliation. After that, the word "courage" lost its meaning, since nothing could be taken from me.

As I continued along the Way, I learned, step by step, word by word, that behind every saying in the Gospels stands *one* man and *one* man's experience. Also behind the prayer that the cup might pass from him and his promise to drink it. Also behind each of the words from the Cross.

Roused from my idle dream,
Freed from all my fetters,
Anointed, accoutred,
I stand ready.

Asked if I have courage
To go on to the end,
I answer Yes without
A second thought.

The gate opens: dazzled,
I see the arena,
Then I walk out naked
To meet my death.

The combat begins: calm,
Yet exultant, I fight,
Until they cast the net
And I am caught.

I have watched the others:
Now I am the victim,
Strapped fast to the altar
For sacrifice.

Dumb, my naked body
Endures the stoning, dumb
When slit up and the live
Heart is plucked out.

July 7, 1960–Spring 1961

June 8, 1961

Body,
My playmate!
Neither the master
Nor the slave,
A buoyant heart
Shall bear you along,
While you cheer my way
With your lively flame.

But body,
My playmate,
You must not flinch
Nor fail me when
The moment comes
To do the impossible.

Sleepless questions
In the small hours:
Have I done right?
Why did I act
Just as I did?
Over and over again
The same steps,
The same words:
Never the answer.

Standing naked
Where they have placed me,
Nailed to the target
By their first arrows.

Again a bow is drawn,
Again an arrow flies,
—and misses.
Are they pretending?
Did a hand shake,
Or was it the wind?

What have I to fear?
If their arrows hit,
If their arrows kill,
What is there in that
To cry about?

Others have gone before,
Others will follow.

June 11, 1961

> Summoned
> To carry it,
> Alone
> To assay it,
> Chosen
> To suffer it,
> And free
> To deny it,
> I saw
> For one moment
> The sail
> In the sun storm,
> Far off
> On a wave crest,
> Alone,
> Bearing from land.
>
> For one moment
> I saw.

June 18, 1961

He will come out
Between two warders,
Lean and sunburnt,
A little bent,
As if apologizing
For his strength,
His features tense,
But looking quite calm.

He will take off his jacket
And, with shirt torn open,
Stand up against the wall
To be executed.

He has not betrayed us.
He will meet his end
Without weakness.
When I feel anxious,
It is not for him.
Do I fear a compulsion in me
To be so destroyed?
Or is there someone
In the depths of my being,
Waiting for permission
To pull the trigger?

July 6, 1961

Tired
And lonely,
So tired
The heart aches.
Meltwater trickles
Down the rocks,
The fingers are numb,
The knees tremble.
It is now,
Now, that you must not give in.

On the path of the others
Are resting places,
Places in the sun
Where they can meet.
But this
Is your path,
And it is now,
Now, that you must not fail.

Weep
If you can,
Weep,
But do not complain.
The way chose you—
And you must be thankful.

July 19, 1961

 Have mercy
 Upon us.
 Have mercy
 Upon our efforts,
 That we
 Before Thee,
 In love and in faith,
 Righteousness and humility,
 May follow Thee,
 With self-denial, steadfastness, and courage,
 And meet Thee
 In the silence.

 Give us
 A pure heart
 That we may see Thee,
 A humble heart
 That we may hear Thee,
 A heart of love
 That we may serve Thee,
 A heart of faith
 That we may live Thee,

 Thou
 Whom I do not know
 But Whose I am.
 Thou
 Whom I do not comprehend
 But Who hast dedicated me
 To my fate.
 Thou—

July 30, 1961

Waking,
Now fully awake,
I heard the scream
That had woken me up.

He had kept watch, floating
Like a drowned man
In the dark depths of the sea,
Rotted by light,
From all directions,
From no direction.

Far away,
For the last time,
I heard the scream,
The scream of terror
The voice of loneliness
Screaming for love.

Who the quarry,
Who the silent hunter
Over the sea of mist
Among the black trees,
Long before dawn?

190

August 2, 1961

"Thou has moved the land, and divided it; heal the sores thereof, for it shaketh." *(Psalm 60:2)*

*

". . . then understood I the end of these men. Namely, how thou dost set them in slippery places; and castest them down and destroyest them." *(Psalm 73:17–18)*

*

"And they remembered that God was their strength—" *(Psalm 78:35)*

*

Almighty . . .
Forgive
My doubt,
My anger,
My pride.
By Thy mercy
Abase me,
By Thy strictness
Raise me up.

ELEGY
FOR MY PET MONKEY,
GREENBACK*

━━

August 6, 1961

> Far from the chattering troop,
> From the green gloom under the treetops
> And the branches over the jungle trail
> Where the eyes of leopards
> Gleamed in the night,
> Alone,
> In the whitewashed room
> With the bannisters and the dangling rope,
> He sat on the window sill
> Watching the snow fall
> And the cars rush by
> With their eyes of fire.
>
> Nobody was watching
> When, one day, he jumped
> For the loop of rope,

---

* The original has no title, but I think that, without one, the reader will be as puzzled by the poem as I was, until I learned the facts. W. H. A.

And his chest got caught in its coils
And he choked to death.
Nobody was watching—
And who had ever understood
His efforts to be happy,
His moments of faith in us,
His constant anxiety,
Longing for something
He could only vaguely remember?
Yet all of us had liked him,
And we all missed him
For a long time.

August 6, 1961

> The meadow's massive
> Green wave rises
> Over the rolling ridge,
> Crested with the white foam
> Of a thousand oxeye daisies
> Which blush
> As the midsummer sun
> Sets scarlet
> In a haze of heat
> Over Poughkeepsie.
>
> Seven weeks have gone by,
> Seven kinds of blossom
> Have been picked or mowed.
> Now the leaves of the Indian corn grow broad,
> And its cobs make much of themselves,
> Waxing fat and fertile.
> Was it here,
> Here, that paradise was revealed
> For one brief moment
> On a night in midsummer?

August 24, 1961

Is it a new country
In another world of reality
Than Day's?
Or did I live there
Before Day was?

I awoke
To an ordinary morning with gray light
Reflected from the street,
But still remembered
The dark-blue night
Above the tree line,
The open moor in moonlight,
The crest in shadow.
Remembered other dreams
Of the same mountain country:
Twice I stood on its summits,
I stayed by its remotest lake,
And followed the river
Towards its source.
The seasons have changed
And the light
And the weather
And the hour.
But it is the same land.
And I begin to know the map
And to get my bearings.

ABOUT THE AUTHOR

With the book *Markings*, Dag Hammarskjöld has left his mark on a generation of readers as an author of great sensitivity who, despite an illustrious political career, never abandoned his spiritual priorities. Known throughout the world as a "peacemaker," his own internal struggles remained a private matter between him and God.

Hammarskjöld felt that *Markings* gave the only true profile of himself. He was born in Jonkoping, Sweden, in 1905 and died near Ndola, Northern Rhodesia, on September 18, 1961, in an air crash while en route to negotiate a cease-fire between the United Nations and Katanga forces. The son of the Swedish prime minister during World War I, Hammarskjöld studied law and economics at the universities of Uppsala and Stockholm. He quickly gained prominence in his own country as secretary and then chairman of the board of governors of the Bank of Sweden before becoming undersecretary of the Swedish department of finance from 1936 to 1945. In 1951 he was made vice chairman of the Swedish delegation to the United Nations, in 1952 he was chairman, and in 1953 he was elected Secretary-General, serving until his death.

His leadership at the U.N. propelled him into that special spotlight of a world diplomat for the cause of peace. His book of meditations has given him further stature as one of the twentieth century's most noted spiritual pilgrims.